MW01630206

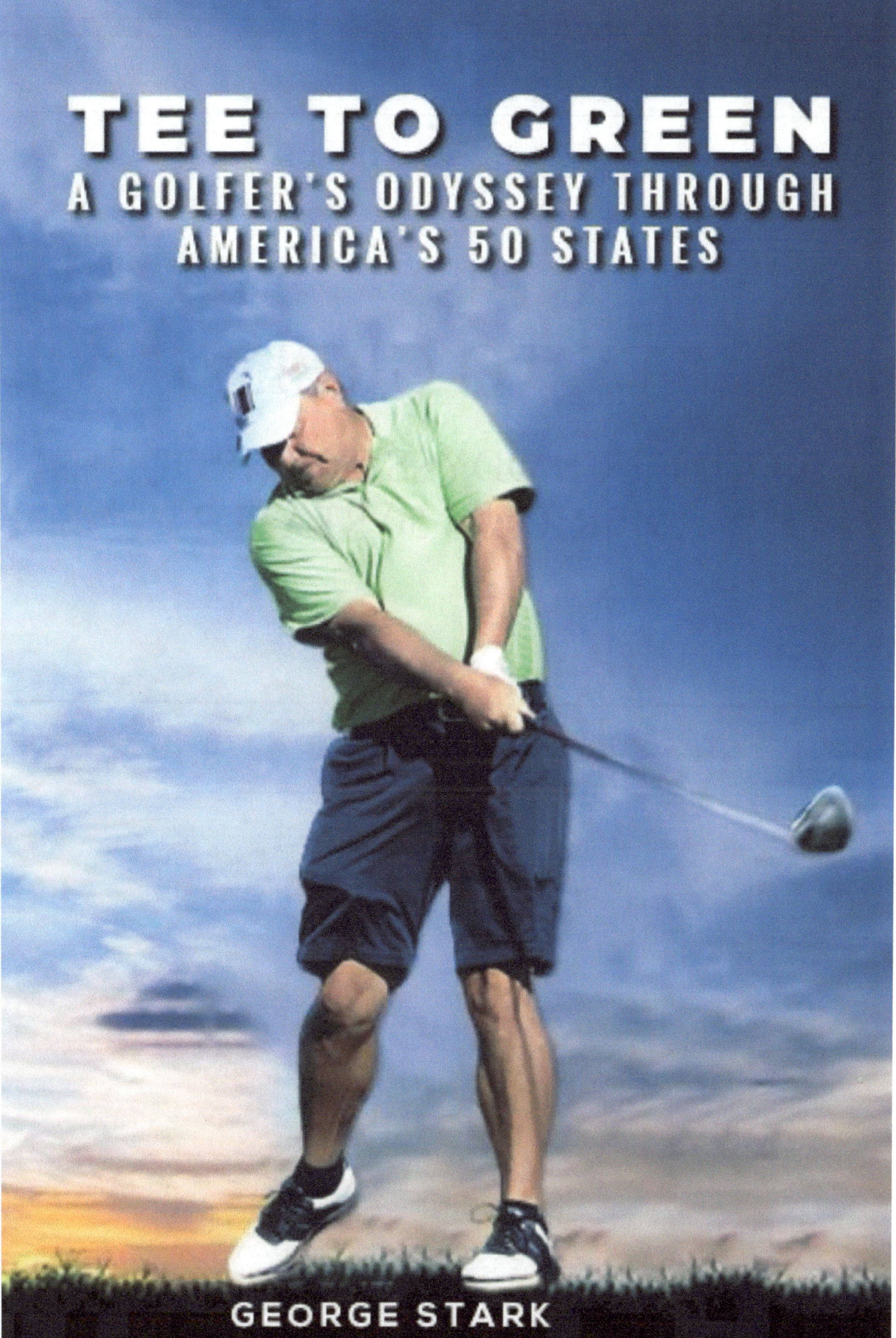

TEE TO GREEN
A GOLFER'S ODYSSEY THROUGH AMERICA'S 50 STATES
GEORGE STARK

TEE TO GREEN

A GOLFER'S ODYSSEY THROUGH AMERICA'S 50 STATES

Table of Contents

Acknowledgements

As I stand on the final green, penning these words to close the chapter on "Tee to Green: A Golfer's Odyssey Through America's 50 States," I am overwhelmed with gratitude for the journey we've embarked upon together. This golfing odyssey would have remained an elusive dream without the support, encouragement, and camaraderie of countless individuals and communities.

First and foremost, I extend my deepest appreciation to my family. To my wife, Patty, whose unwavering encouragement and understanding allowed me to chase this lifelong dream, and to my children, Jeremy and Kelley, whose love and patience kept me grounded throughout this journey. My brothers, Mark, Mick, and Dan that took me to play many interesting and fun courses. My sister and brother-in-law, Betty and Kevin, for help with photo tips and enhancements when needed.

I have an amazing group of friends that like to travel and play golf. We have adventured together across all 50 states and enjoy the variety of courses in the United States. Blake Johnson has been with me to 26 states, Kevin Kliefoth, 17 and Peter Thompson 15.. My good friends Larry Sartin, Norm Ogrin, Barton Gill, and Sam Rodriguez have all assisted in helping me reach my goal. Jim McCausey and his son Trey who hated my driving so much that I was banned after a few hours behind the wheel on our road trip to finish the 50 states in Kentucky and Indiana. Pat Wilson whose continual encouragement to "write this down," motivated me to finish the book. We have played some great courses and some not-so-great courses together, but we always had fun and enjoyed the journey.

Friends and colleagues Brian Campbell, Daniel Yates and Steve Bayer who went out of their way to find old pictures from our times together and help me remember courses that we played. Their contributions were immense for this book.

My friend Bill Moretti is in the Texas Golf Hall of Fame and is one of the Top 50 instructors in the United States. He has taught dozens of tour pros as well as a few Presidents. I always enjoy his company, his humble energy and the time he donates for all my whims including reviewing drafts of this book and helping me to play some incredible courses. Another pro that has given me a lot of his time and helped me in achieving this goal is Glenn Lee. Glenn is a great ambassador for the game and has helped me play fantastic courses. I am honored to spend time playing and talking with the awesome men about courses, statistics, and the personalities that shape golf.

My great friend Laurie Jones has provided amazing encouragement and spent many hours proof reading and formatting these pages several times. This work would not exist without her effort. My niece, Laurin Macios helped me with the publishing process based on her experience in publishing two books.

I want to acknowledge the people I met on the fairways and in the clubhouses across America's 50 states. The fellow golfers who shared their stories, their passion, and their local insights enriched this journey immeasurably. Especially my friends, Paul and Brad, from Pennsylvania that I met at Oglebay in West Virginia; Jeff and Kevin, two great guys from Waverly Woods in Maryland; the gang in the pub at Fox Hollow in Delaware, all were highlights of my adventure. We all enjoyed post round drinks and good conversation about the area. Your camaraderie reminded me that golf is not just a sport but a bridge that connects us all. As my great friends Bill Askins and Cliff Baize used to say "90% of Golf is who you play with."

To the golf course owners, managers, and staff who welcomed me with open arms, often providing guidance on the best places to eat and explore in their respective regions, thank you. Your hospitality and warmth made each state feel like a home away from home.

Finally, to the readers who embark on this golfing odyssey through the pages of "Tee to Green," thank you for your interest and enthusiasm for the sport and for exploring America's diverse golf courses with me. With your support and the support of all those mentioned here, I can truly say that this journey from tee to green has been an unforgettable odyssey. Thank you for being a part of it.

Sincerely,

George Stark

Tee to Green: A Golfer's Odyssey Through America's 50 States

Introduction

The first time I played golf was my 12th birthday in July 1973. My sister's boyfriend, George Bray, took me to play nine holes at our local municipal course, "City Park" in Pueblo, Colorado. We played the "Short nine" (nine holes, par 30) across the street from "The Big Course", now called Elmwood Golf Course. I was terrible. Shot 70 on the nine holes, but I was hooked!

Elmwood Golf Course #18, Pueblo, CO

My Sister-in-law's Dad gave me a mis-matched starter set with a 2 wood, 4 wood, 3-5-7-9 iron and a putter. The woods were different, the irons were all different brands, but I played the rest of that summer, every day. My Mom would give me $1 per day for me to play as many holes as I could on the short nine as well as get a hot dog and a coke. I rode my bike the short distance with my clubs over my shoulder. It was a great place to grow up and learn the game.

As I got better, my mom and dad bought me a matched set of Lord Byron golf clubs from Kmart. The set contained a Driver, 3-wood, 5-wood, 3-PW irons and a putter. It was awesome! I tried to find a picture of these, but several searches online proved fruitless. My high school coach, Ken Lewis, fixed my grip and taught me to hit a draw. My parents then purchased a set of MacGregor Tourney VIP irons for me in 1979. These were very nice clubs, actually from a pro shop. I had hit the big time! I played with these irons in the Insurance Youth Classic, one of the largest junior tournaments in Colorado at the time. Ah, but that was a long time ago.

I realized I would never be a professional golfer in high school and turned to math and statistics instead. I worked as a research scientist for the MITRE Corporation supporting NASA and NORAD. Then as a data scientist for the IBM Corporation. I currently hold more than 25 patents and have published more than 40 technical papers on software measurement and data science… I'm a bit of a data nerd. I have kept several years of spreadsheets full of rounds played with hole-by-hole scoring, fairways and greens hit in regulation, scrambling percentages from different distances and lies (e.g., fairway, rough, sand, fringe), ball played, environment conditions and course rating and slope. When my wife passed away in 2019 and I retired from working, I needed a goal. I reviewed my list of courses that I had played and decided to finish the goal of golfing in all 50 states.

My handicap fluctuates between three and six, in the no man's land of golf … not good enough to play with the scratch players and not enough strokes to play in Net (handicap) events. At 62 years old, I hit it pretty short, carry about 240 off the tee and hit my five-iron about 180 yards, so, I rarely play the back tees… 6,500 is good yardage for my game right now. I have been playing now for 50 years … I'm still hooked.

This book is a compilation of some of the courses that I have played in each state. There is some inconsistency in the documentation by state and course because I completed this adventure over the past 50 years. In my early days I did not always take many pictures of the course or even remember some of the rounds, but I logged each course I played. There have been more than 500 in eleven countries. During the last five years I have been much more diligent in recording the rounds and photographing the adventure (thank goodness for cell phones).

As I spoke with people about the idea of writing this book a few common questions emerged:

- What was your favorite state?
  - o Oregon, no doubt. Bandon Dunes, Bandon Crossing, The Reserve Vineyards, Pumpkin Ridge (both courses), Eugene Country Club, and even Pine Ridge and Cross Creek were fun to play, interesting layouts with great hazard placement and wonderful staffs.
  - o South Carolina. A close second with Myrtle Beach and Hilton Head. Great cities for golf. I prefer Hilton Head since both Harbour Town; Haig Point are incredible and there is a bevy of outstanding courses in close proximity. Additionally, it is a short drive to Kiawah Island.
- What was your favorite course?
  - o Hard to beat Sand Hills in Mullen, NE. The fact that we met Ben Crenshaw there and he played in the group ahead of us made it even more special.
  - o Bandon Dunes in Bandon, OR. The rankings of the Bandon Courses are a personal choice, but most people I talk with that have been there have Pacific Dunes and Bandon Dunes neck and neck. I give the nod to Bandon after four visits. I believe it has great shot values, a good set of par 3 holes and with the weather is still playable.
- What is your least favorite?
  - o None. I love golf and have a great time wherever I am. The courses mentioned in this book are the ones that I played and enjoyed, many times because the course or experience itself was quirky. Most times though it is because of the friends or newly made acquaintances on the first tee. Ninety percent of golf is about who you play with.
- Desert or Mountains?
  - o Yes, please. I love playing the desert. Desert courses in California, Arizona and even Wisconsin. The flight of the ball against the blue sky is fun to watch. The lack of trees made it easier for a low-ball player like me. I love playing in the

mountains. Colorado, California, Vermont -- all have spectacular mountain courses that can boost your ego one second with a 300+ yard drive and crush your soul the next as your putt rolls off a green by thirty yards down the mountain. The ball goes far and high in the altitude.

- Links or Parkland?
  - o I prefer links golf to parkland golf. Kind of silly for me to live in Central Texas where Parkland is the norm, but the links courses in Florida, Oregon, South Carolina, even Michigan and New York leave you with a WOW! You just don't get in a parkland setting in Chicago, Columbus, or Dallas.
- Most important lessons
  - o Swing Easy and Accept the Extra Distance. A mantra that I started using when my kids were born, and I wanted to teach them the game. It serves me well and reminds me to slow down when I get excited.
  - o 90% of Golf is who you play with. The is from good friends, Bill Askins and Cliff Baize. As I have grown older this indisputable truth has become the central theme in this book. You will read it many times within these pages…

I believe golf courses are some of the most beautiful places on the planet. The large green spaces, wildlife, lakes and plant life make for a pleasant walk or ride every time. I have taken most photos in this book, although a few were sent to me by friends that I played with and a very few of the photos come from internet searches. I hope you enjoy reading the book as much as I did golfing the courses and writing about my odyssey.

Alabama

Alabama entered my golf consciousness in 1978 when I visited my brother who was stationed at Gunter AFB in Montgomery. While there, he took me to play the two courses at Maxwell AFB as well as Bonnie Crest Country Club. Bonnie Crest was closed in 2013, after nearly 70 years in business. For most golfers, Alabama Golf was thrust into the spotlight with the 1990 PGA Championship at Shoal Creek. That tournament is famous in the United States for the protests surrounding the club more than the tournament. Shoal Creek is a club in Birmingham, AL and at the time had no African American or minority members. Various groups threatened to protest the event and sponsors pulled out, and the PGA considered moving the tournament away from Shoal Creek. The TV show Nightline produced a segment on the controversy. The podcast <u>Local Knowledge</u> produced a well balanced view of the event called The Reckoning at Shoal Creek. In the end, a local African American executive accepted an invitation to become an honorary member and the tournament was held as planned. Wayne Grady, an Australian, won by three shots over Fred Couples.

Today, Alabama is famous for The Robert Trent Jones Trail, a set of 26 Golf Courses with 468 holes in 11 locations across the state. I have played several courses on the trail, but not all. Of those I have played, my personal favorite is The Judge in Prattville, just north of Montgomery. Capitol Hill Golf Center, home of three courses, The Judge, The Senator, and The Legislator, was named the #2 public golf facility in the country by Golf World readers. Additionally, GOLF Magazine called the Judge course one of the 10 public courses in America worthy of hosting the U.S. Open. Also, the Zagat Survey of America's Top Golf Courses ranked it among the top 50 courses in America. It is that good.

The Judge offers amazing views along the backwaters of the Alabama River. The first tee lies 200 feet above the fairway overlooking the river and the Montgomery skyline. With 14 holes adjoining the water and a bulkheaded island green, The Judge is magnificent. Better bring your A game because there are many forced carries and numerous bunkers. It is long (7,813 yards from the tips), we played it at 6,500 and it was a beast and hard (slope rating of 131). The 650+ yard 7th and the 700+ yard 11th are beastly par 5s that require strength and strategy. The 7th requires a long straight tee shot over a lake and the 11th second shot must negotiate two enormous bunkers. I am also a fan of the 18th, a short, uphill par 4 with a waterfall along the right side.

Course: The Judge

Type: Public

Website:

https://www.rtjgolf.com/capitolhill/

Location: Prattville, Alabama

Phone: 334-285-1114

Par 72.   Yardage Played 6577 (Orange Tees).

Rating 71.7/131

Scenes from the first hole at The Judge

A few of the forced carries at The Judge

Alaska

Alaska is a huge state. It is 665,400 square miles with more than 33,000 miles of tidal shoreline. In my twenties and early thirties, I worked for a Federally Funded Research and Development Center (FFRDC) supporting the US Air Force out of Peterson Air Force Base in Colorado Springs, CO. As a Radar engineer, I was primarily responsible for three radars in the inventory: Princlik, Turkey, Thule, Greenland and Shemya, Alaska. Both Princlik and Shemya had rudimentary 3 hole "courses" around the radar. I played the three holes. Several of my friends gave me grief about Alaska when I discussed writing this book. The comment, "you didn't post a score", so Alaska doesn't count. So, in July of 2023 Laurie Jones and I flew to Anchorage for a week to play "championship" golf courses and post some scores.

We were looking forward to seeing some of Alaska's booming wildlife population (e.g., bald eagles, moose, fox, waterfowl and bear). Unfortunately, while we were shown a couple of videos that our playing partners had taken on the courses, we were shut out except for a few ducks and one Bald Eagle. We did get to see some of Alaska's wildlife population while visiting a conservation area a few days later.

Our first day in Anchorage we played the number two course in the state according to Golf Digest, Anchorage Golf Club (or O'Malley's as the locals call it). Anchorage Golf Club was the host to the 2022 US Women's Senior Amateur and was in excellent condition when we visited. With this event, the United States Golf Association (USGA) has hosted an event in all 50 states as well as Washington DC and Puerto Rico, which I thought was cool.

It was an overcast July day of 62 degrees with little wind, pretty much perfect. As we arrived, we were greeted with the U.S. Senior Women's Amateur sign and a golf bag that was turned into a planter. A novel idea we may adopt when we get home with a spare bag or two. The driving range at Anchorage Golf Club was large and had a great view of the mountains with the clouds sitting well below the peaks. This was an interesting contradiction, with the course being at sea level and the mountains thrusting skyward. The legendary Denali can be seen on a clear day from many vantage points throughout the course.

Course: Anchorage Golf Course

Type: Public

Website:

https://www.anchoragegolfcourse.com

Location: Anchorage, Alaska

Phone: 907-522-3363

Par 72. Yardage Played: 6601 (Black Tees).

Rating 71.4/129

After the first hole, a short par 4 with a bunker in the driving area on the right, it was difficult to find a level lie other than the tee box. Seriously, Anchorage Golf Club, played like a mountain course, lots of uphill, downhill, and side hill lies to contend with and large trees to navigate… but we were at sea level. The 4th is a picturesque dogleg left, downhill par 4 of 425 yards. Off the tee, the 4th has a very large mound on the left making the tee shot blind, and if you don't hit it around the corner, you are laying up. Once you negotiate "the hill", there is a pond guarding left and behind the green and a bunker on the right side, the second shot requires precision to make a birdie.

Anchorage Golf Club was the best course we played in Alaska for conditioning, shot value and green complexes.

Scenes from Anchorage Golf Club

The Creek Course at Moose Run was a good layout and ranked by Golf Digest as the #1 Course in Alaska as of June 2023 (https://www.golfdigest.com/places-to-play/collections/alaska-best-golf-courses-rankings). The raters had clearly not recently been to the course. Moose run had had a difficult winter and spring. The fairways were marked with patchy grass and a lot of dead areas. The greens were bumpy and needed some TLC. The bunkers needed to be loosened and trimmed on the edges. Overall, the conditioning was subpar and made Anchorage Golf Club look like Augusta National. It was important to swing easy and accept the extra distance.

Course: Moose Run
Type: Public
Website:
https://www.mooserungolfcourse.com
Location: Anchorage, Alaska
Phone: 907-384-4653
Par 72. **Yardage Played** 6,230 (White Tees).
Rating 70.6/133

The Creek Course is one of two courses open to the public on the Joint Elmendorf-Richardson U.S. Military Base. The other being the Hill Course. The Creek Course is the longest golf course in Alaska at 7,324 yards from the back tees, and has the Longest Single Hole, the par 5, number 11 at 640 yards (I played it from 520). We were paired with Jung H., an incredibly nice man that had lived in Anchorage for 30+ years and who was preparing for the Arctic Open to be held the next weekend at Moose Run. He hit the ball a long way off the tee and was incredibly helpful in navigating the course. When we mentioned that we had not seen any wildlife, Jung showed us a video of a black bear coming out of the trees on the 9th green to steal his Gatorade and Scotty Cameron Putter from his cart a few weeks ago. He also told us that the bears had learned the sounds of the different golf carts in use at the course and would only come around when the "player" carts were there, not the marshal or course maintenance carts.

Moose Run has a 30 yard wide very fast-moving creek racing through it. The military recently erected two bridges to help navigate the course, they were certified to 8,000 lbs. Not sure why a four-ton capacity bridge was needed, but it was a smooth ride in a golf cart. The 9th and 10th holes at the Creek Course were very good holes. The 9th is a 500-yard par 5 that has a landing area about 240 out, just short of a native area (310 to clear) and a second one another 220, just short of the creek. There is also a large tree on the left leaving a small landing area for the second shot to have a short 80-yard pitch to the green over the creek. The 10th is an uphill 400-yard par 4 that requires a tee shot back over the creek and short of the native area leaving a 200-yard approach to the green. Getting through these two holes lead to the longest hole in Alaska, the 640-yard par 5 11th.

Scenes from Moose Run

Views on Moose Run

Our flight didn't leave until 8 pm, so we spent an afternoon at Jack Russian Municipal in Anchorage. This is a unique property as all the tee boxes and all the greens are artificial turf. The

Fairways were long park grass in a while that hadn't been mowed. With a par of 31 (5 par 3s, and 4 par 4s), it cost $8 to play nine holes, it was silly and fun. The tee boxes would hold a tee but the greens would not hold a shot. It was crucial to roll the ball onto the turf slowly. The turf greens were hard and ran about a 15 on the stimpmeter[1], lightning fast. I was lucky enough to chip in three times on the back nine to win the beer from Laurie. If you have an hour and need to hit a golf ball, do it and have fun!

	Course: Russian Jack **Type**: Public **Website**: https://www.muni.org/Departments/parks/Pages/Russian_Jack_Springs_Golf_Course.aspx **Location**: Anchorage, Alaska Phone: 907-343-6992 **Par** 31. **Yardage Played** 1,977 **Rating**: Not Rated	

---

[1] Stimpmeter is a device used to measure the speed of greens on a golf course. It is really a piece of plastic with a slot for a golf ball. The person measuring the speed lifts the stimpmeter up until the ball rolls down the ramp. Three balls are rolled in each direction on a green. The average distance the six balls travel is the speed of the greens. Most greens run about an 8, on the PGA tour they are 12-13.

Scenes from Jack Russian

Arizona

Arizona is known as "The Grand Canyon State" and "The Copper State." The Grand Canyon is one of the world's natural wonders and the park itself is bigger than the state of Rhode Island. Arizona is the nation's leading producer of copper. The Copper Queen mine in Bisbee, Az has an outstanding mine tour (the mine itself was closed in 1975). Arizona has between 260 and 320 days of sunshine per year making it a tremendous golf location. With more than 300 courses across the state, Arizona possesses links, parkland and target golf courses to challenge your skills and provide you with some unbeatable fun. The first time I played in Arizona, I had just turned 16 and was playing chess in the United States Open Chess Championship. I was about the same talent level as a chess player and golfer. My talent was okay, but not a master. The US Open Chess Championships are conducted over a two-week period in August with one game played each evening, which was cool, leaving all day for golf! Although, golf in Phoenix during the month of August is scorching hot!

The hotel that hosted the tournament was close to Papago Municipal Golf Course. In 1977, the all-day rate was something like $10, so I played all day, mostly alone because of the 105-degree temperatures. It was pretty much heaven for a 16-year-old golf nut. Since then, the course has gone through a few renovations, but it is still highly regarded in the Phoenix area for a municipal course. The price has gone up too. It is now $120 for out-of-town guests according to their website. (https://www.papagogolfclub.com).

As a young adult, my first job out of college was in Sierra Vista, Arizona. While living there I often played the courses on the U.S. Army post (Fort Huachuca) and the daily fee course, Pueblo del Sol; My wife and I often visited the Copper Queen mine in Bisbee and the OK Corral in Tombstone. We never paid to see the world's largest rose bush there. On occasion, we drove to Tucson to play golf and go to the movies. Ventana Canyon was my favorite although El Rio golf course, host to the Tucson Open for 18 years was fun too.

Papago Golf Course

Recently, my friends and I did a buddy's trip to Scottsdale. We played Anthem Country Club (Ironwood Course) and Gainey Ranch Country Club (all three nines) through our Invited membership. We also played McDowell Mountain and Red Mountain Ranch based on recommendations from friends.

The Ironwood Course at Anthem is one of my favorites. It is a wonderful desert design that blooms well in March and April that plays to more than 7,250 yards from the back tees. We played the blue tees at 6,400 and had a wonderful time. The Ironwood par 3's are visually stunning and tough. They vary from 140 to 217 yards with water, sand and Saguaro cactus guarding the greens and tees! The par 5's are a mixed bag with a couple of very long ones (570 yards) to very short (486 yards). A good set of par 4's long and short with dog legs and straight-aways. The greens are large with a lot of undulation. They day we played they were running close to 12 on the Stimpmeter and were a challenge to two putt. The course is full of quail, prairie dogs, bunnies and a big ole owl that watched over us during the round.

Course: Anthem Country Club - Ironwood Course

Type: Private

Website:

https://www.invitedclubs.com/clubs/anthem-golf-country-club

Location: Anthem, AZ

Phone: 623-742-6200

Par 72. Yardage Played 6,425 (Blue)

Rating: 71.0/134

A few shots from Ironwood Course at Anthem Country Club

Wildlife and Saguaro full of Golf Balls

Desert Golf at its Finest

Arkansas

Arkansas is known as "The Natural State." It claims home to more than 125 golf courses from the Ozark mountains in the northern part of the state all the way down to the Arkansas Delta where cotton is still a major crop in the southern part of the state. Two courses that opened in 2004 are Blessings, designed by Robert Trent Jones, Jr and Alotian by Tom Fazio. These two courses garner most headlines in the state. Blessings was built by the Tyson Chicken family as the University of Arkansas home course. The Razorbacks host many collegiate events and rank highly in the nation because of the test provided by this layout.

Alotian is near Little Rock overlooking Lake Maumelle. The course is very hilly but has underground heating and cooling system to keep the bent grass greens running smooth throughout the year. The club is very private, and some have compared it to Augusta National. Alotian is currently ranked #38 in the United States by Golf Digest.

Personally, we played Mystic Creek in El Dorado, Arkansas. Originally an oil boomtown, El Dorado is headquarters to Murphy Oil which owns the course. Developers were starting to build homes around the course when we played, hopefully they do not spoil the natural beauty of the tall pines and scenic water features. Mystic Creek was voted best new course of 2013 by Golf Digest and voted the #1 course you can play in Arkansas by Golfweek.

Our buddies' trip to Mystic Creek was a comedy of errors. First my good friend Blake noticed that he lost his wallet when we made our first stop for gas on the trip. A frantic search of the car, golf bag and luggage turned up nothing. Then he called his neighbors and asked them to go look in his house. Nothing there either. Luckily Blake had just set his phone up with Apple Pay and used his phone to pay for most of the trip. Isn't Technology amazing. Where the merchants did not take Apple Pay, we covered him. Second, my good friend, Peter, booked our hotel for the wrong night. He had booked it for the week after we arrived. Fortunately, there was availability at another hotel in town at a substantial price increase, but at least we were able to get lodging. Finally, I booked our tee time at Mystic Creek for the wrong day! This was an interesting conversation with the pro. Luckily, there was a light mist and several people canceled their time on the day we showed up and we were able to play, at double the cost since there was no refund for our pre-paid missed tee time the day before. Sometimes things just don't go right, but the goal was still achieved, played an excellent course and have a good story.

The Mystic Creek golf course is excellent! Designed by Kenneth Dye, Jr. it has cathedral pines similar to Augusta National, domed greens with runoffs similar to Pinehurst #2, and high flashing bunker styles similar to A.W Tillinghast. Mystic Creek is tough from all sets of tees, but can be stretched to 7,500 yards for the professionals out there. Tee Boxes, Fairways and Greens are all Champions Bermuda which is perfect for the heat and humidity of the south. Mystic Creek starts and ends with par 5 holes that are fair and birdieable. The par 3's holes vary in distance ranging from 140-210 yards meaning every club gets tested.

Course: Mystic Creek
Type: Public
Website: https://www.golfmysticcreek.com
Location: El Dorado, AR
Phone: (870) 312-0723
Par 72. Yardage Played 6,723 (Green)
Rating: 73.5/137

My favorite holes were #3 and #10. Three is the #1 handicap hole playing a little over 400 yards with water down the left and an "S" shaped fairway. Hitting your tee shot down the right (but avoiding the trees) will leave a longer approach to a huge green. Challenging the water on the left will leave a shorter approach; be sure to miss the deep bunker on the right of the green.

Views at Mystic Creek

Number 10 is another 400+ yard par 4 with water down the right side. It is best to hit your tee shot to the left center side of the fairway, anything right side will run into the water. The approach requires a long to middle iron towards two-tiered green which slopes from left to right and is protected by water on the right. A steep faced bunker guards the left side of the green and a long narrow bunker protects the right side of the green next to the water. Any two of the collection areas that face the front of the green will collect shots that land too short.

Most of the holes at Mystic Creek will challenge every skill level. It is worth the trip.

Bunkering at Mystic Creek

California

California is an amazing state for golf and golfers. It is the third largest state in the United States by area (behind Alaska and Texas), but California's 840 miles of coastline are spectacular. The weather varies significantly from San Diego in the south to Crescent City in the North. California has both the lowest point in the US (Death Valley) and the highest point in the contiguous 48 states (Mount Whitney). There is excellent golf in these areas, in fact, as of 2022 there were 921 golf courses in California.

Pebble Beach in the Carmel Valley is consistently ranked as one of the top 3 courses in the United States by all major ranking publications with Augusta National and Pine Valley. In addition to Pebble Beach, Olympic Club, Los Angeles Country Club, Riviera, Torrey Pines, Harding Park, and Hillcrest Country Club have all hosted Men's Major Championships. I have played many of these along with others in both Northern and Southern California. La Quinta, Indian Wells, and others in the desert as well as Incline Village in Lake Tahoe.

A couple of gems that I still remember from when I was younger were Elkins Ranch in Fillmore and the Eisenhower Course at the City of Industry. Elkins Ranch was built in 1961 out of an avocado and orange grove. It was a short course by today's standards but played much longer than the 6270 yards on the scorecard because of the narrow fairways and the Kikuyu grass fairways and greens limited roll. Elkins Ranch was closed in 2020 because of the cost of maintenance and the COVID pandemic.

I played The Eisenhower course at the CITY OF INDUSTRY in the early 1980s with persimmon woods and Macgregor irons. It was a long course that was well maintained. It had hosted US Open qualifiers. I remember clearly the second and ninth holes. The second had great views of the San Gabriel mountains from an elevated tee and the ninth was a short par 3 from which you drove your cart into an inclined railcar to take you up the hill to the tenth tee. It was fun and memorable!

My daughter took me to the Farmers Insurance Open in 2018, Tiger Woods first tournament back after his very public breakup with his wife, Elin. We had a fabulous time walking with Tony Finau, watching Phil, Ricky and Beau Hossler.

Course: Torrey Pines - South

Type: Public

Website:

http://www.torreypinesgolfcourse.com

Location: San Diego, CA

Phone: (858) 452-3226

Par 72. Yardage Played 6,635 (Green)

Rating: 73.3/134

I had also played the North Course later in 2018 after doing some work with San Diego County government but did not get to try my hand at the South Course until 2023. The South Course has hosted several Major Championships and the weekend rounds of the Farmers Insurance open for more than 50 years. It did not disappoint. It is long, with the ocean breeze wreaking havoc on several shots. Spectacular ocean views, hang gliders circling the beach, and enjoying the day with lifelong friends; it couldn't be better. My friend since I was 15 years old, Duane and his wife Jennifer joined me and a wonderful lady, Laurie for the day.

William Bell (the original architect of Torrey Pines South) and Rees Jones (architect for renovations in 2001 and 2019) both did a fabulous job routing the course both inland and oceanside. Since it's a public course, I recommend every golfer get there at least once.

Scenes from Torrey Pines South

I really enjoy golfing in the desert. The warm sun, well-manicured greens and tees, pretty water features, palm trees and cactus. The California Desert contains a lot of small towns with spectacular golf. As a Texan, I lump them all together as "The Desert", but I was corrected several times by locals that they are vastly different places. I have played golf in Palm Springs, Palm Desert, Rancho Mirage, Indian Wells, Indio, and La Quinta. I suppose there are several other locations in the California desert that I have missed, I'll fix that in the future.

Mission Hills was home to the LPGA's Dinah Shore (Chevron Championship) for 51 years, a major championship on the LPGA tour and the place where it is tradition for the winner to jump into the pond on #18. Amy Alcott started this tradition in 1986. They have multiple courses at Mission Hills.

We played the Palmer Course. I like Arnold Palmer designs. They are playable, interesting and fun. The Palmer course at Mission Hills has a lot of water on holes 9-16, it is not difficult to navigate, but it can drown golf balls that are mishit.

Course: Mission Hills - Palmer
Type: Private
Website:
https://www.invitedclubs.com/clubs/mission-hills-country-club
Location: Rancho Mirage, CA
Phone: 760-324-9400
Par 72. Yardage Played 6,484 (Blue)
Rating: 71.2/127

My favorite hole at Mission Hills was the short par-4 12th. It is a big dogleg right around a lake that provides some fun shots. Be careful not to pull your ball through the fairway or you might find another lake hidden on the other side. The 17th is an fun an challenging 170-yard par 3 with water guarding the green short, as well as sand traps guarding the left and right sides of the green, the only play is the center of the green.

Scenes from Mission Hills Country Club

I really like the logo at Indian Wells. The arrow in the ground at the first tee and the totem pole 150-yard markers make me smile. The course was originally owned by Desi Arnez and Lucille Ball and played host to the Bob Hope Desert Classic for more than 45 years. It is the course where, in 1995, Former U.S. Presidents George Bush, Sr. Bill Clinton, and Gerald Ford played together with Scott Hoch and Bob Hope for the Chrysler Classic. This course helped get the PGA Tour to where it is today. I thoroughly enjoy that the club has not lost this history and has memorabilia all around the clubhouse. The course itself, is somewhat short by today's standards and could not host a professional event with today's equipment and bombers on tour. It is fun to play for us shorter hitters and people that are interested in golf history.

Course: Indian Wells

Type: Private

Website:

https://www.invitedclubs.com/clubs/indian-wells-country-club

Location: Rancho Mirage, CA

Phone: 760-345-2561

Par 72. Yardage Played 6,496 (Black)

Rating: 72.1/130

Some Memories from Indian Wells History with Golf

Colorado

As my home state, colorful Colorado rarely disappoints. It has stunning views, beautiful rivers and lakes and is mountain golf at its finest. The elevation helps to make you feel like a bomber and the trees reverberate the "WHACK" into your soul. I simply love Colorado golf. There are ego boosting courses like the 9 hole municipal course in Estes Park to humbling tracks like Castle Pines and its 7,700 yards with a course rating of 76.0 and slope of 147.

Elk on the Estes Park Course

When I was a high school player, the 1978 US Open came to Cherry Hills in Denver. My friends and I drove the 110 miles from Pueblo for the day. Andy North won. That was the first time I saw REAL golfers. These guys hit towering drives, crisp irons, and it was incredible to watch. It gave you a sense of how the game is supposed to be played.

Castle Pines Golf Club

Later that summer, the LPGA had an event at Columbine Country Club. We drove up for that one too. We followed Silvia Bertolaccini, an Argentine golfer in her late twenties for 18 holes. We were the only three in her gallery. She was phenomenal! After the round she gave us all the golf balls in her bag and signed a glove for each of us. She talked with us for probably 20 minutes and was just a wonderful lady. It didn't hurt that she played well that day and moved up the leaderboard.

I have played more than 60 courses in Colorado, including the more famous ones like Cherry Hills, Arrowhead, the Broadmoor, and Castle Pines; but my home track, the one I grew up on, was City Park Municipal in Pueblo. It has 27 holes, an executive nine that is par 30 and the 18 hole "big course" as we called it as kids. The name was changed several years ago to Elmwood, and I still travel back twice a year for the Memorial Day Two-Man and the Labor Day Championship to play with my brother. It is a comfortable place. It is where I first broke 100, 90, 80 and 70. It is nothing spectacular or a must play, but it is home.

Course: Elmwood

Type: Public

Website:

https://www.pueblo.us/1002/Elmwoo
d-Golf-Course

Location: Pueblo, CO

Phone: (719) 561-4946

Par 70. Yardage Played 6,624 (Blue)

Rating: 69.5/117

My favorite hole at Elmwood is the second. It is a tough dogleg left 420-yard, par 4 with tall cottonwood and elm trees guarding the left-hand side from tee to green. The green has two tiers and is guarded on both left and right by bunkers. A par here is a good score. My least favorite hole is the 110-yard 4th. This hole was part of a redesign with the third. As a kid, both the third and fourth holes were short, tight par 4s that demanded a well-placed tee shot through, over or around trees. The approach to the 4th was straight downhill. It demanded focus and thoughtful club selection. The holes are now a par 5 and a par 3 with greens that are too small and do not fit the design of the rest of the course. The 4th is no longer scenic and feels cramped. It has two pot bunkers that are "old school" (i.e., natural, unpredictable, and unkept) and the green is far too hard and narrow requiring a lot of luck to make a par from such a short distance. I have aced the 11th and 14th at Elmwood, both were playing about 165 yards when my shot went in, and both were with a 7-iron.

My brother and I have played the Memorial Day two-man event together at least 25 years. We have won it a few times, but the favorite memories are feeding the squirrels peanut butter crackers out of the golf cart and watching the deer as dusk approaches. A lot of good feelings here.

Views of Elmwood

Views of Elmwood

Connecticut

Connecticut is New England's second smallest and southern-most state. Its 5,018 square miles (13,023 square kilometers) are bordered by New York State on the west, Rhode Island on the east, Massachusetts on the north, and by Long Island Sound on the south. It is roughly 117 miles across, making it an ideal location to play golf in multiple states in a single day or on a quick trip. Our little group flew into Hartford from Austin, Texas and played in Connecticut, New Hampshire, Maine and Vermont on a very quick trip. We also went to a Rhode Island seafood festival that was amazing!

Fresh Lobster Rolls are Awesome!

We played two courses in Connecticut. The first was the Player course at Lyman Orchard. If you like quirky, this course is for you. The front nine has multiple blind shots, requires crisscrossing around the same holes a few times, ensuring you must hit away from the final target at times, and rarely using your driver because, well, there's a hazard there. 🤣😆. The back nine has a couple holes cut through an apple orchard. Not sure what Gary Player was thinking when he routed this course. Most par 3's were from elevated tees and very picturesque. Two par 5's to finish the round. Strange, but memorable. The course was in excellent condition and the staff was incredible. It was also fun to play with my former boss, Paul Manore, and my good friend, Peter Thompson. Both Paul and Peter are good players that had a good day at Lyman Orchards.

Course: Lyman Orchard – Players

Type: Public

Website:

https://lymangolf.com

Location: Middlefield, CT

Phone: 860-349-6000

Par 72. Yardage Played 6,325 (Blue)

Rating: 71/130

Lyman Orchards Logo and Friends

Views at Lyman Orchards

The second course we played in Connecticut was The TPC at River Highlands. This is one of the private TPC courses in their portfolio. We were able to get a tee time through a friend who was a professional at the TPC Summerlin, another private TPC course in Las Vegas. The TPC River Highlands is famous as the course where Jim Furyk shot 58 in a tour event. Here is a photo of his scorecard that hangs on a wall outside the restaurant/bar at the course.

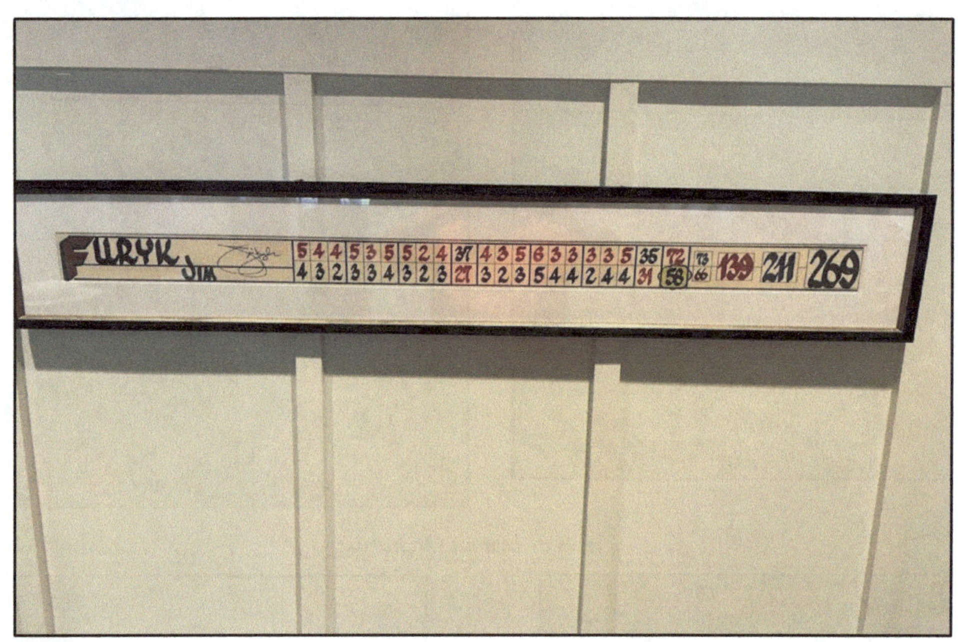

Jim Furyk Scorecard for round of 58

Course: TPC River Highlands

Type: Private

Website:

https://tpc.com/riverhighlands/golf/

Location: Cromwell, CT

Phone: (860) 635-5000

Par 70.   Yardage Played 6,518 (Blue)

Rating: 71.5/127

Trust me when I tell you, this course is NOT that easy. The greens we large with some false fronts. My buddy, Blake, who is a solid 6 handicap, putted it off the green on the first hole after barely missing on the low side. I hit the ball well and shot 82. It was a phenomenal experience. The course played long for me and my friends as it was very wet and there was very little roll.

Another cool feature of the TPC River Highlands course is the ring of champions near the driving range. Here is an example plaque from the ring. I chose George Archer because I had played with him on my home course in the Georgia Pacific Super Seniors Pro-Am which was part of the Kinkos Classic in Austin, Texas. Our team with George Archer won that day with a score of 49! Yes, you read that correctly, 49! The format was one best ball net, Shamble. He was a fun guy to play with that even at 64 could really work the ball and had an incredible touch around the greens. He told us several fun stories, including his response to a San Francisco Golf reporter who said he would never amount to a very good player. George sent him a copy of that article after he won the Masters with a red FU on it. Made us all laugh, then he signed my Masters Flag.

George Archer Ring of Champions Plaque and Signed Masters Flag

Scenes from TPC River Highlands

Delaware

Delaware is small. It is only 96 miles long and ranges from 9 miles to 35 miles across, giving a land area of 1,982 square miles making it the second-smallest state in the United States after Rhode Island. By Comparison, Alaska, the biggest state is 665,400 square miles.

On December 7, 1787, Delaware became the first state to ratify the Constitution of the United States and has since been known as "The First State." Since the turn of the 20th century, Delaware is also a de facto onshore corporate haven, in which by virtue of its corporate laws, the state is the domicile of over half of all New York Stock Exchange-listed business and over 60's of the Fortune 500.

There are only 50 golf courses in Delaware. Frog Hollow is a relatively new course that opened in 2000. It was designed by Allen Liddicoat and Dave Horn. It quickly rose in the Golf Magazine and Golf Digest rankings becoming the #1 Course in Delaware in 2009. More recently it has had a few issues with the sprinkler system (hit by lighting) coupled with drought conditions that left the course in rough condition for a couple of years. I played it recently (in October 2022). It has come back and boasts the title of "best public golf course" in Delaware.

Course: Frog Hollow
Type: Public
Website:
https://www.froghollowgolfclub.com
Location: Middletown, DE
Phone: (302) 643-2918
Par 71. Yardage Played 6,608 (Blue)
Rating: 72.1/128

The course has a links-style layout that is challenging but still player-friendly enough to appeal to beginners, seniors and juniors. The layout is wide open and quite forgiving but there are still plenty of hazards with which to contend if your tee ball strays. The course is fairly short on the front nine at only 3,080 yards, but the back makes up for it at 3,528. I booked a tee time on GolfNow and was paired with three beginners. They were very nice guys who understood they were learning the game, but it made for a long day. The tall rough off the fairway shown in the next picture had interesting sticky pods in them. It is paired with a picture of my pants after searching for one of my playing partners balls for about 2 minutes roughly five yards off the seventh tee.

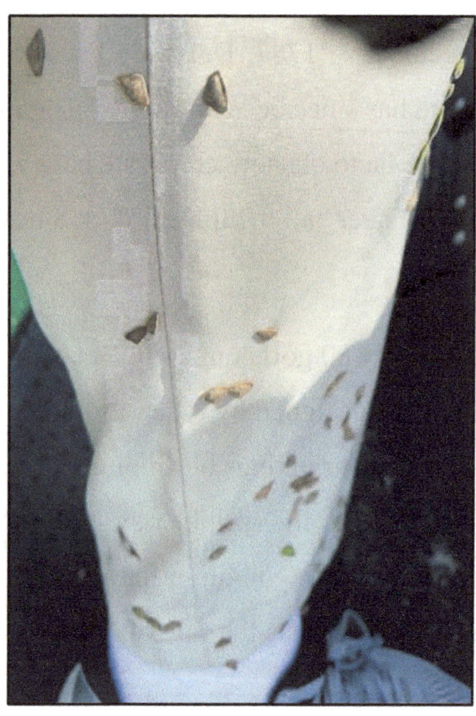

The Rough and Stickers at Frog Hollow

Frog Hollow has more than 50 strategically placed bunkers throughout the golf course. Their thoughtful placement makes up the bulk of the layout's challenges. There are ponds that come into play on six holes as well as tall native grasses that appear along the fairways and greens. The wind is often a factor on the course too and will test your accuracy even further. The Frog Hollow Golf Club par 3's and par 5's are manageable, but the par 4's will test even the best players.

Views at Frog Hollow

There were a lot of geese on the course in October, when I played. To keep them off the greens and reduce the amount of manure from the geese, the course has employed several high-pitched sound devices as shown in the picture. Evidently these things emit a very annoying sound to the geese that keeps them in the pond and in the fairways, but off the greens.

The par 5 eleventh is a really good hole that is shown here. A long tee shot down the right side can get you in position to get home in two, but a miss either left or right is trouble. The second shot is either a layup short of the hazard or over the bunker. The fairway is split by the heavy rough. It is a well designed hole.

Tee and Approach to the Par 5 11th hole

After the round I went into the clubhouse to grab some lunch. I met a group of members that were very welcoming. We talked about my quest to play in all 50 states and we talked about their course. They were very passionate about Frog Hollow and about golf. They bought me a couple of beers and told me about the history of the course, one of the guys was the current course record holder at 63. I would highly recommend this course to anyone in the area.

Florida

Florida is an amazing golf state. More than 1,250 courses are in Florida, ranging from the panhandle's Perdido Bay Course in Pensacola to the Key West Golf Club (the southernmost golf course in the US). Seminole is widely considered the best course in the state, also the most private.

I have played only 21 of the 1250, but my favorite so far is the Belleair Country Club near Clearwater. This is the oldest course in Florida and an incredible Donald Ross design. I was lucky enough to get an invite through the Society of Golf Historians on Facebook! The restoration of this course is documented in a fun book written by Hal Bodley (founder of MLB Network and former baseball editor of USA Today). The book documents the 125-year history of the Belleair CC.

Course: Belleair CC - West

Type: Private

Website:

https://www.belleaircc.com

Location: Belleair, FL

Phone: (727) 461-7171

Par 72. Yardage Played 6,448 (Blue)

Rating: 71.2/132

Jason Straka, the course restoration architect used many original documents to recreate the fantastic look and feel that Donald Ross intended. Trees and lakes were removed and replaced with a meandering creek and large dunes throughout the course. The greens are very large with mounding and ridges throughout, meaning local knowledge plays a large role in approach shots. Placing your ball in the wrong spot on these greens will leave a difficult three putt. 😉

I was able to play Belleair thanks to Facebook! Society of Golf Historians founder and Belleair member, Connor Lewis, decided to host an event to show off his club and invited people on Facebook to play. I was lucky enough to make the trip from Texas for the event. I was paired with two outstanding Floridians. One an orthopedic surgeon and the other a sports memorabilia dealer. They shared wonderful stories about their life and careers, and we enjoyed a great day on a beautiful course. One of the highlights after the round was a podcast with Connor, Hal, and Jason. After the podcast, they hosted a trivia contest for the few of us that stayed. It was fun! I won an Augusta National hat and ball marker and an Oakmont putter cover for being the first correct answer on three separate questions!

The 5th hole at Belleair CC

Across the Dunes at the 7ʰ Hole

Some views of the bay at Belleair

Trivia Winnings and Playing Partners

Georgia

Ah, Georgia. The Peachtree State. The Okefenokee swamp is the largest in North America. Okefenokee translates to trembling earth and all kinds of critters like alligators, snakes, turtles and birds can be found in its several thousand acres. But for golfers there is only one thing in Georgia... Augusta National, the REAL start of the golf season … The Masters. I have been to four Masters, but never played the course. I can say this: It is really long and very hilly. TV does this no justice. My friend Brian and I never found a weed on the course; we looked for several hours. Here are some pictures from one of the Masters that I attended. The iconic scoreboard and the 16th hole where during practice rounds the players skip it across the water along with Amen Corner #11 green, #12 green and #13 green. Very fun.

But I digress, this is a book about where I have actually played, not where I dream about playing… that would be a much longer book. Georgia has about 350 golf courses. Some are incredibly nice and some, well, not so much. I have played only a handful and in both categories.

My favorite that I have played is Eagle's Landing Country Club in Stockbridge, GA. This is a parkland course with 27 holes designed by Tom Fazio. It was used by Georgia State University as a practice facility until the Bobby Jones course opened in 2019 for them. The plantation-style clubhouse at Eagle's Landing exemplifies Georgian charm looking down on a beautiful pond and around the 18th green. Brian and I stopped to play here on our way to The Masters in 1998. It was a good choice.

Course: Eagle's Landing CC
Type: Private
Website:
https://eagleslandingcc.com
Location: Stockbridge, GA
Phone: (770) 389-2000
Par 72. Yardage Played 6,636 (Blue)
Rating: 72.5/132

Brian and Me in front of the Clubhouse at Eagle's Landing

The courses created by combining the nines are "normal" length by today's standards (6,900 from the Championship and 6,400 from the tournament tees), but there aren't any skinny fairways, unfair landing zones, or hidden obstacles/hazards. The rough is manageable and the bunkers are well maintained. The course plays longer than the yardage because it is often very soft. The Lake 9 has a lot of casual water, especially on the first two and final three holes. If you are a 10+ handicap or not a long hitter, consider playing from the member tees. The Creek 9 has two long par 3's, 190+ to the back pin, and Lake 9 has two 200+ par 3's. The course was in amazing shape when we played the first week in April and I would recommend it to anyone in the south Atlanta area.

Views of Eagles Landing

Hawaii

Hawaii is magnificent! Every Island has its own terrain and beauty. The Big Island has 12 separate climate zones. Kauai is the Garden Isle and has remained relatively undeveloped. These are fun places. My favorite, however, is Maui. Nicknamed "The Valley Isle," due to the great valley that lies between its two major volcanoes, Maui is known for its stunning natural beauty as well as its high-end luxury resorts and popular tourist attractions — a triple threat ranking the island among the world's top vacation destinations.

The Royal Ka'anapali Course is one of only two courses in all of Hawaii designed by Robert Trent Jones, Sr. The architect took advantage of the rolling landscape to create sloping fairways and large contoured greens to ensure a challenging approach to each hole. Golf Digest Ranked the course as a 100 Greatest from 1969-'74. The course was also part of Golf Digest's original 200 Toughest Courses list from 1966-'68.

Course: Royal Ka'anapali

Type: Resort

Website:

https://www.kaanapaligolfcourses.com/the-royal-kaanapali-course

Location: Lahaina, HI

Phone: (808) 661-3691

Par 71. Yardage Played 6,700 (Blue)

Rating: 71.8/129

Royal Ka'anapali is situated on Maui's northwest side—a short drive from Kapalua—with terrific views of nearby Lanai and Molokai. The course plays over varied terrain, starting on the coastline before moving into the foothills of West Maui Mountains. Though the course tips out at a modest 6,700 yards, strong trade winds often present a stern test.

18th Green at Ka'anapali

The Royal Ka'anapali Course begins at sea level with a par 5 hole extending 550 yards. The course hugs the shoreline before winding its way to the West Maui Mountain foothills. Arnold Palmer called the 18th hole (par 4) one of the best and most challenging finishing holes he'd ever played. The 449-yard hole plays longer than it looks, hugging the brackish water canal the entire length of the fairway and green, making it a memorable last hole.

I played this course in December of 2000 with my good friend Bob Packer. We enjoyed the views and talked about his company, Packeteer, that was about to go public. Bob believed in "relative scorekeeping", whatever I made on a hole he took one more, unless he beat me on the hole in which case, I made a double bogey by definition. It was a fun round.

18th Green at Ka'anapali

The beautiful history of this course is presented to you as you make your way around. Each tee has a historical plaque, sharing the history and stories of Ka'anapali. The course will take you Makai (Oceanside) and then bring you into the West Maui Mountain foothills (Mauka) with stunning panoramic views. Sloping vistas reveal the islands of Lanai and Molokai in the distance. You will see rainbows that remind you that this course is a special place. Be mindful of the trade winds that keep you cool during your round and look up to the palms for windspeed and direction.

Historical marker with great views

Idaho

Idaho is a stunningly beautiful state. Idaho is famous for its potatoes, but the state's nickname is "The Gem State" because of the abundance of rare minerals that have been found throughout the state. In fact, more than 70 different gems can be found there. The Star Garnet is the most abundant, but there are also Amethyst, Opals, Sapphires and Topaz in Idaho. One of my good friends, Paul Oman, has been a professor at the University of Idaho in Moscow for several years. He and I published a few papers together through the years and met at several conferences. One of those was at the Coeur d'Alene resort. WOW! Designed by Scott Miller, this is a fun golf course with mounds on sides of the fairways that act like bumpers in bowling… most drives end up in the fairway. The forecaddies are funny and helpful. It is a treat to have them with the group.

Course: Coeur d' Alene
Type: Resort
Website:
https://www.cdaresort.com/
Location: Coeur D'Alene ID
Phone: (855) 703-4648
Par 71.   Yardage Played 6,497 (Black)
Rating: 71.6/124

In fact, I was met at the jetty by our caddy who showed us around. First stop was the driving range where piles of floating, monogrammed balls are available to hit into the lake. Then we were taken up to a masseuse who gave a wonderful back, head and shoulder massage before we teed off. It was pretty cool.

Driving Range at Coeur d'Alene

The par 3 holes on this course are phenomenal. Built on the site of an old sawmill, the course at the Coeur d'Alene resort is most famous for the floating green on the par three 14th hole where the distance from tee to putting surface is changed every day by computer control. The green extends to around 15,000 square feet so some might argue there's no real excuse for missing the target. Golfers complete the hole by boarding an electric powered shuttle boat and when they return, today golfers are presented with a certificate to mark the completion of this rather unique hole. When I played it in 1996, I missed the green into the bunker short right, but made a good par. I rewarded myself with a bag tag. My Buddy Glen played the hole recently, hit the green and got his certificate!

My buddy Glen with his Certificate and view of the 14th Hole at Coeur d'Alene

Perhaps the most stunning view on the course is overlooking the lake from the 3rd tee box. This 150-yard par 3 is picture postcard stuff. It should be in a painting, for sure.

The 11th is the best par 5 on the property, in my opinion. It requires a well-placed tee shot followed by the decision to layup or challenge the greenside bunker. Birdie is makeable here.

Number 11 at Coeur d'Alene

Coeur d'Alene has three par 3 holes in the first six! The back-to-back 5th and 6th are fun. The 5th is a short 120-yard hole with a three-tiered green in the shape of a clover and two-thirds of it is protected by a large bunker. This is a classic sucker hole. Trust me, go for the middle of the green, regardless of the pin location. Finally, the sixth hole, often referred to as the other signature hole, is another par 3, 150 yards, all downhill. Don't let the picturesque view dull your golf senses and watch out for the ball-eating junipers on the right.

The "other" par 3s at Cour de' Alene

Illinois

Illinois is a big state. Chicago is the third largest city in the USA and the biggest in Illinois. The Sears Tower (now called the Willis Tower) is the tallest building in the United States at 110 stories (1451 feet). Illinois produces more nuclear energy than any other state. It also has more than 770 golf courses. Chicago has more than 200 golf courses with several famous clubs. One of the most highly rated public facilities in the United States is Cog Hill.

I must admit, I felt a touch of nervous excitement as I stood on the first tee at Cog Hill #4, the fearsome "Dubsdread" course that hosted 20 PGA tour events since 1991. Originally Designed by Dick Wilson & Joe Lee, the course was built to test the world's best golfers. A redesign in 2011 by Rees Jones was intended to keep the course relevant for today's longer hitters. My friend, Glenn Daly and I had made the trip to Chicago on our way to Dubuque, IA for work. One of the most demanding courses in the US, Cog Hill #4 had received a lot of criticism from the tour professionals, including Phil Mickelson and Steve Stricker for the changes that were made.

> *"There's really no shot-making here that's required," Mickelson said of the BMW Championship host course. "It doesn't really test our ability to maneuver the ball because the fronts of the greens are blocked, and the only shot is to hit a high flop shot that stops. Chipping areas, shot value around the greens, penalties for certain misses, all that stuff wasn't really well thought out."*
>
> *--Phil Mickelson on Cog Hill #4*

Course owner Frank Jemsek, who spent $5.2 million on the renovation in 2011 does not agree with the critics.

> *"Phil and I have a difference of opinion," Jemsek said. "I like Rees' work. I'm not saying that I like the work just to justify my hiring of the guy. I like that he made big greens into three small greens because we were trying to make the golf course more challenging and put the 'dread' back into Dubsdread."*

The former host of the Western Open, and BMW Championship is located in the southwest suburbs of Chicago, about a 40-minute drive from O'Hare airport. Dubsdread is consistently ranked around number 50 in the top 100 public, and most difficult courses in America. My friend, Glenn, sent me a Facebook post reminding me of our round at Cog Hill #4, with the ranking of best in Illinois in 2012.

Course: Cog Hill #4

Type: Public

Website:

https://www.coghillgolf.com

Location: Lemont, IL

Phone: 866.264.4455

Par 72.   Yardage Played 6,750 (Blue)

Rating: 74.2/140

---

* Jeff Rude, Hate to be Rude: Lefty rips Cog Hill makeover, Golfweek, September 15, 2011

The view off Cog Hill #4

For me, the individual holes were not very memorable, they were similar in that they were long, tree-lined and had challenging carries into big greens with a ton of bunkers. I walked away not remembering much of the routing but overall impressed with the course difficulty and conditioning. It had deep rough and narrow fairways for a parkland layout. The course was intimidating… off the tee due to numerous fairway bunkers forcing various carry distances or shot shapes. The intimidation continued as the greens were well protected with deep bunkers, and were large, undulating greens that placed a premium on landing zones. For these reasons, I tend to agree with Phil on his assessment of the course, it is built for bombers and floppers. Guys that play low running shots or rely on putting to score are at a big disadvantage here. It made me realize how great Tiger's course record of 62 is, especially considering the pros played from 7,554 yards versus the 6,750 we played. Long story short, give it a play if you are in the area and make your own decision!

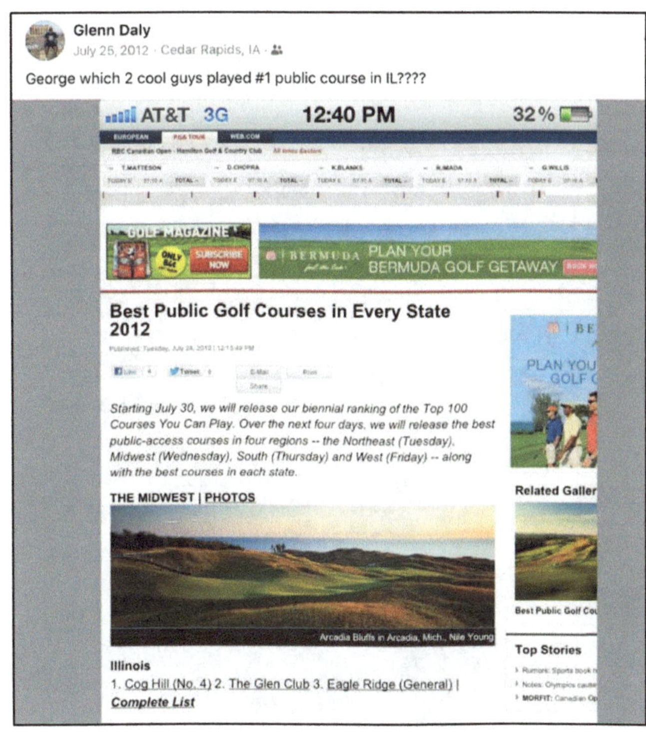

A Facebook Post from my Friend Glenn Daly about our trip to Cog Hill #4

Cog Hill #4, Dubsdread

69

A couple of the more difficult shots at Dubsdread

Indiana

Ah, the Hoosier state. Home to Bobby Knight and everything basketball. The movie Hoosiers with Gene Hackman is one of my favorites, even with all of its editing faults. Indiana has some famous golf personalities, too. Masters Champion, Fuzzy Zoeller and Short Game Guru, Dave Pelz played their college golf there. The amazing golf course designer, Pete Dye, is from Indiana. John Daly shocked the golf world, when, as 9th alternate, he won the PGA at Crooked Stick in 1991 with drives farther than many had ever seen. Yes, Indiana is important to the golf world.

The PFAU course at the University of Indiana in Bloomington is one of the most difficult courses I have ever seen. It is very long. Nearly 8,000 yards from the tournament tees. There are a few forced carries, a 147 bunkers to navigate with huge greens (some of them are mowed square, which is fun) that have numerous pin placements to make any day memorable.

Course: The PFAU Course

Type: Public

Website:

https://thepfaucourse.com

Location: Bloomington, IN

Phone: (812) 855-7543

Par 71. Yardage Played 6,736 (Blue)

Rating: 74.3/147

The PFAU course has a couple of wonderful short par fours with a collection of trees forming a gallery on many tee shots. The zoysia fairways are framed first with 8-10 yards of bluegrass rough followed by a blend of fescue, or Irish links, that is reddish/orange in color and significantly enhance the already picturesque views throughout the course. The Irish links rough is wispy and designed to allow golfers to find and play their ball from it, which I did several times.

Opened in 2020, The PFAU course at Indiana University was built on the same 265-acre east side Bloomington property previously occupied by the IU Championship Golf Course, the original Par-3 course, and the IU Cross Country Course since the 1950s. It is currently ranked as the #5 course in Indiana by Golf Digest. The course is NOT for the faint of heart. It has blind shots, doglegs and a great set of one-shot holes. The 7th and 15th were both set back the day we played, close to 250-yards playing up hill. The par fives are for the big boys, do yourself a favor and play one or two sets up.

As a side note, this course completed my 50th golfing state. Jim mentioned this in the pro shop prior to our teeing off and the head pro gifted me the ball marker in the photo to commemorate the occasion.

Road Trip to University of Indiana with my friends Jim and Trey McCausey

Views at the PFAU Course at Indiana University

Views at the PFAU Course at Indiana University

Iowa

Iowa is the only state bordered by two navigable rivers; the Missouri River to the west and the Mississippi River to the east. It has been said that "Iowa feeds America"; Iowa ranks first in beef, pork, corn, soybean and grain production in the United States. In addition to being the home state of Ryder Cup player and captain Zach Johnson, Iowa has at least 437 golf courses for recreation during the summer months. In the summer of 1978, a couple of friends and I decided to drive from Pueblo, CO to Chicago, IL to play in the United States Open Chess Championships. This is about 1,100 miles. Our car died in Williamsburg, Iowa. We were 850 miles from home with 250 miles to go. We decided to take the bus, it picked us up at a Texaco station … we had a five-hour layover, so I went to the 9-hole golf course. That was fun.

More recently, I worked in Dubuque, Iowa. It is a unique town on the Mississippi River basically bordering Wisconsin and Illinois. They have 4 courses in Dubuque, one of which is private. I played Bunker Hill, the municipal course, and the Meadows golf course a couple of times each. I played Bunker Hill in late October when they were hosting a "Big Hole" tournament, evidently this is common in the colder parts of the United States for the winter months. The hole was cut on an edge of the green that was not usable during "normal" play and was about 10 inches in diameter. It made chipping and putting fun! Also, if you're in town for a big hole event, it probably means the women's roller derby is in town and can be a fun evening event.

Big Hole Tournament at Bunker Hill, Dubuque, IA

The Meadows course is on a nice piece of rolling property and the Bob Lohmann design uses the natural contours. This leads to some challenging greens and a lot of uneven lies. The Meadows was in excellent condition, and the bent grass greens rolled true. The course was soft when I played, making it play longer than the yardage, but easier overall. The Meadows is an open layout, with few obstacles to hinder a bombs-away strategy. The holes are generally straight, and the fairways generous with few trees. The difficulty in the course comes from two things: negotiating the hills and the wind. The course changes direction and has subtle and severe slopes that force you to review ball position in your stance with every approach shot. The wind seems to come from every direction.

Course: The Meadows
Type: Public
Website:
https://meadowsgolf.com
Location: Dubuque, IA
Phone: (563) 583-7385
Par 72. Yardage Played 6,457 (Blue/Black Combo)
Rating: 71.0/121

The sixteenth is a 388-yard par 4 from the tees we played. It was a favorite. The locals call it "The Dolly Parton Hole" because of the two mounds that must be negotiated on either side of the fairway. A well-placed tee shot splits the mounds, leaving severe downhill second to a green located on a hill with a creek behind. We were encouraged to hit 3-wood because a solid drive leaves a tricky downhill lie. Club selection on the second shot needs to be managed as it plays at least a club and a half downhill. The Meadows is a good course should you be in the Dubuque area.

Views of the Meadows Course in Dubuque

Kansas

Kansas is known as "The Great Plains." It is mostly flat farmland dotted with oil wells. It is home to Dorothy from the Wizard of Oz as well as scorching summers, freezing winters and big tornados. The geographic center of the lower 48 United States is located about 2.6 miles northwest of the center of Lebanon, Kansas. Kansas has some great golf. Prairie Dunes in Hutchinson has been ranked in the Top 50 in the United States (currently 23rd) since Press Maxwell added 9 holes to his dad's original 9 holes in the 1950s. I have never had a chance to play there. My personal favorite that I have played is Lionsgate in Overland Park.

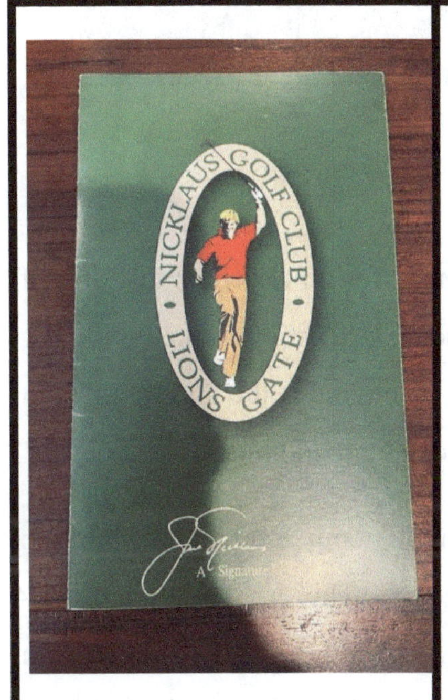

Course: Lionsgate CC
Type: Private
Website:
https://www.invitedclubs.com/clubs/nicklaus-golf-club-at-lionsgate
Location: Overland Park, KS
Phone: 913-402-1000
Par 72. Yardage Played 6,689 (Blue)
Rating: 73.1/136

The Golf Club at Lionsgate, a signature design by Jack Nicklaus, is an 18-hole championship course. It is the only links-style private club in the Kansas City area. Built in 2001 with Zoysia grass fairways and bent grass greens, the course is always in excellent condition. Unlike some Nicklaus designs, the fairways are wide, no undue penal golf here. Well-placed bunkers- most noticeably centerline pots ahead of the greens – enforce the risk/reward challenge. The greens are a good size with slopes and several pin positions (some of them very difficult for higher-level play).

Two tee shots highlighting the centerline pot bunkers

The variety of holes and the different challenges they present make for an excellent test of golf. Bunkering is well placed and can be in play on almost every shot. In addition to the bunkering, tall native grasses and a few water hazards add to the challenge. The wind is the biggest factor at Lionsgate. With the mix of uphill and downhill holes, the wind can help and hurt dramatically.

According to a Golf Digest article, Jack told his audience during his course opening exhibition, that he patterned some holes after ones he has admired in the past. The drive-and-pitch par-4 seventh was inspired by the 15th at Rhode Island Country Club, a Donald Ross design he and son Gary had played just a few years earlier. He said the par-3 eighth is his salute to the infamous Redan Hole at Scotland's North Berwick (although few would recognize it as such), and the very attractive 447-yard 11th was a variation of the 13th at his own Muirfield Village Golf Club. Not much like it, he admitted, as Muirfield's plays uphill, while this 11th plays downhill. It was the shot requirements of the Muirfield hole he tried to instill. And the slick bank of closely mowed turf feeding off the 13th green and into a bunker was obviously a nod to Augusta National.

A Friendly Hawk watching us play the 14th at Lionsgate

Both sides of the course end with par 4's of similar length, running alongside each other back to the clubhouse. The ninth hole uses a pair of fairway bunkers to make reaching in regulation difficult while the 18th hole uses a line of fairway bunkers to dare players to bite off as much as they think they can chew if they want a birdie putt.

Views on Lionsgate

Kentucky

Kentucky is a great state. Horse Racing, Bourbon, Basketball and Golf. What more could a guy want? I was lucky to enjoy two stellar private clubs in the Lexington area: Triple Crown Country Club and Traditions Golf Club. These two courses were fabulous, and they served wonderful local bourbons in the clubhouse bar. I can't thank my friend Jim and his son, Trey, and their buddy Mike enough for a wonderful time in Kentucky.

Traditions Golf Club, in Hebron, a few minutes south of Cincinnati has been ranked as one of the best courses in Kentucky by Golf Digest: It has been ranked inside the top 5, 1997-2001 and inside the top ten 2003, 2007, 2011, 2012, 2015, 2016, 2019-2023. Traditions Golf Club had the lowest cumulative handicap index of any club in Kentucky and has hosted the Big East Championship.

Course: Traditions CC

Type: Private

Website:

https://www.traditionsgolfclub.com

Location: Hebron, KY

Phone: 859-586-6691

Par 72. Yardage Played 6,773 (Blue)

Rating: 72.5/141

The 20th anniversary golfer statue in the roundabout as you enter the club sets the tone for the day. Swing away and go low. There is very little trouble off the tee. The green complexes make this course a challenge for all skill levels, they are smooth, quick and can have some diabolical pin placements if the superintendent gets up on the wrong side of the bed.

The holes that I remember most vividly are the 9th and the 17th. The 9th is a hard dogleg left around a set of large trees. If you hit it high, you can bomb it and get close to the green which is elevated with levels that force you to hit a controlled iron to the correct level. The 17th is a downhill par three with water and sand. It is very picturesque and can lull you into a quick double-bogey if you miss hit your iron off the tee.

Memorabilia before starting at Traditions

Views at Traditions Country Club

Views of Traditions Club in Hebron

Triple Crown Country Club, in Union Kentucky, opened in 1990 and has hosted the Kentucky Amateur and the Greater Cincinnati Open. Designed by Gene Bates, it has been a "Best in State" course by Golf Digest several times: Ranked inside the top five in 1993, 2003, and again in 2017-2018. Ranked inside the top ten in 1995-2001, 2005-2007, 2013-2016. 2019-2020. Our host, Mike B., is a great guy. As the owner of his own law firm, he was able to get away to spend the day on the course and have some bourbon. It was a good day.

Course: Triple Crown CC

Type: Private

Website:

https://www.triplecrowngolf.com

Location: Union, KY

Phone: (859) 384-1410

Par 72. Yardage Played 6,434 (Derby)

Rating: 71.6/136

The course was in immaculate condition for early May with its tee markers named Belmont, Derby, and Preakness. We played the Derby course because it had been raining and there would be no roll. It is in a residential setting, but you really don't feel the houses like many courses. Many holes dogleg right to left, with only two (9th and 10th) favoring a fade. Hitting a draw on Triple Crown is an advantage.

The course has a creek that fills several ponds all of which come into play and force decisions on club selection that can be uncomfortable. The first hole starts you off downhill dog leg left with a creek hugging the left side. This 400-yard par 4 requires a tee shot to the right making the second shot a little longer to an undulating green that slopes back to front. Don't be above the pin, it is lightning fast down that slope.

Triple Crown Country Club

The 510-yard par 5 10th hole has a pond off the tee and down the right side until it crosses in front of the green to force a couple of decisions. First, how close to the pond do you want your tee shot, second, go/no go to get to the green in two, third, how far left do you hit your second shot if you lay up and finally, how hard to hit your third over the lake if you successfully laid up on the 2nd shot. It is exhausting to concentrate on each shot. The entire course is this way, few holes where you can take a breather and make a simple par.

After the round, the bar is fantastic. Enjoy golf in Kentucky and have a local Bourbon that you cannot get out of state, like Michter's. The people are friendly, and the golf, bourbon, and horses are wonderful.

Views at Triple Crown Country Club

Louisiana

Louisiana, the Pelican State, is a fun state. It has a state dog, after all (the Catahoula Leopard Dog), how great is that? Baton Rouge, the state capital, is one of the best places to tailgate for a college football game. The music, food, and fun in New Orleans is spectacular. Gambling in the casinos in Shreveport and many other Louisiana cities is entertaining. There is good golf in Louisiana too! There are less than 100 golf courses in Louisiana, but they are exciting to play. A group of us went to the Koasati Pines Resort in Kinder, a short five-hour drive from our base in Austin, assuming you don't run into an accident on I-10 in either Houston or Louisiana.

Course: Koasati Pines

Type: Resort

Website:

https://www.coushattacasinoresort.com/golf/

Location: Kinder, LA

Phone: (337) 738-4777

Par 72.   Yardage Played 6,571 (Blue)

Rating: 71.3/127

We rented a limo for our group and a truck to take our clubs and luggage, a good way to travel! A couple of guys from the Limo company wanted to go to the Casino for the weekend, so they gave us a discount for the trip, so we made it a "guys and gals" excursion.

The tee markers are dice in reference to the casino on property. The landscaping is top notch and the area between the clubhouse and driving range is great for photo opportunities. Unfortunately, because of all the recent rain, the course itself was water-logged, and it was cart path only. It is a long walk with cart path only. Koasati Pines can be a beast from the back tees, playing 7,600 yards in wet conditions with very little roll. It is the longest course in Louisiana. From the "regular" tees it plays 6,700 yards bringing several lay-up shots short of water, sand and throw a few alligators into the mix. Better have a good short game, especially if the greenskeeper has a bad night.

For this trip we had both men and women playing and competing in a Quota-Stableford format on the course. The Quota-Stableford format gives players points based on their score on a hole. In our case, 0 for double-bogey, 1 for bogey, 2 for par, 4 for birdie and 6 for Eagle. There is also a -1 penalty for triple bogey. A player's Quota is 36 minus their handicap. The winner of the event is the player with the most points over his/her Quota.

Our ride and destination

Kevin Tucker, the course architect, created a consistent and solid layout. In my opinion, the course could have used a drive-able par 4, more variable yardage on the par 3's (3 of the 4 played right at 200 yards) and more options around the greens. It is a bombers course that rewards hitting the ball high and being able to hit flop shots near the greens. There are few places to run the ball up onto the greens.

The 12th hole is a memorable par 3 with an island green and the back-to-back par 5's (9 and 10) can be brutal. From where we played (Blue) it felt like the course was tougher than what is reflected on the scorecard, even with the ample driving areas. The par 5 9th at 527 yards, is one of the better holes because of a hazard short of the green and fairway layup areas on both sides of the hazard.

The course also has a 19th "gambling" hole designed to help settle wagers and break ties. Distance ranges from 85 yards to 175-yards on this Island green par 3. It is a fun way to end the day and head back to the casino.

Two holes at Koasati Pines showcasing the water carries

Some of our gang at Koasati Pines

Maine

Maine is known for its stunning ocean views and great lobster, both are amazing! As for golf, Maine has some of the most challenging and scenic New England golf courses.   The Pine Tree State has more than 100 courses. There are golf courses overlooking the ocean in York and at Samoset, some are surrounded by lakes and rivers while others are nestled in the mountains with dramatic views like the golf clubs at Poland Springs, Sunday River and Sugarloaf.

We were lucky enough to be invited by a friend to play Webhannet Golf Club in Kennebunkport. As a semi-private golf club Webhannet has limited tee times available for visitor play. Monday through Wednesday has one tee time per hour. No tee times available Thursday through Sunday. This is a fantastic Donald Ross course built it in 1901. The greens were quintessential Ross, turtle backs and subtle undulations. The rough was thick and deep. An incredibly fair test with clear sight lines and excellent hazard placement.

Course: Webhannet Golf Club

Type: Private

Website:

https://www.webhannetgolfclub.com

Location: Kennebunk, ME

Phone: (207) 967-2061

Par 72.   Yardage Played 6,100 (Blue)

Rating: 69.0/120

The day we played, holes 2 and 3 were interesting in that 2, "Burnside", played as a tight 300-yard par 4, while 3, "Needles' Eye," was a long 248-yard par 3. I hit driver off the tee on both and was lucky enough to go birdie-par. "Burnside," is a short dogleg left with out-of-bounds on the left. Since I'm a pretty short hitter, I did not have to worry about driving through the fairway on the right. The green is steep back to front, so it was relatively easy to keep my approach below the hole. "Needle's Eye", is the longest par 3 on the course. The card shows 238, but it was measuring 248 yards from the back tee the day we played. Over-swinging was an option, but that certainly would have resulted in the ball finding the left-side hazard. The green slopes right to left and can be quite fast.

Peter, Blake, and I had an amazing day with challenging shots and difficult greens. If you get a chance to play Webhannet, do it.

Welcome to Webhannet Golf Club

Views on Webhannet

Some Tee Shots at Webhannet

Some Approach Shots at Webhannet

Maryland

Maryland is known for crab cakes and a very busy state flag. Baltimore is the major city and is known for the National Aquarium and Edgar Allen Poe's House. Chesapeake Bay is a popular spot for crabbing and Lexington Market is one of the oldest markets in the United States. Waverly Woods Golf Course in Baltimore is an Arthur Hills design and is the home course for the Baltimore Ravens of the National Football League. It also maintains a Golf Academy with a fantastic practice facility. Waverly Woods is in Howard County, Maryland which claims the 7th highest median household income in the United States. It has been ranked as one of the top courses in Maryland for several years (2022 #11) (2021 #4) (2020 #11) (2019 #15) (2018 #11) (2016 #12) by Golf Digest.

Course: Waverly Woods
Type: Public
Website:
https://www.waverlywoods.com
Location: Marriottsville, MD
Phone: (410) 313-9182
Par 72.   Yardage Played 6,602 (Blue)
Rating: 72.2/132

Named "Best of Baltimore" by Baltimore Magazine. "Among the finest in the region" according to Golfstyles Magazine. "A Must Play" wrote the Washington Times. Play Waverly Woods Golf Club, a Golf Digest 4 star rated public golf course that the Baltimore Sun hailed as "rivaling the area's most elite clubs". Arthur Hills used the gently rolling, wooded terrain, added very few bunkers, but focused on small undulating greens to demand focus from the golfer. A signed picture of a young Fred Funk hangs in the clubhouse. Fred is a native of Maryland and was the golf coach at the University of Maryland before making his way on tour in 1989. One of the straightest hitters on tour, he won The Players in 2005.

I flew into Baltimore and signed up as an individual with GolfNow. Upon arrival I was paired with two great guys, Jeff and Kevin. I was lucky in this pairing in that all three of us were about the same handicap and we hit the ball about the same distance.   They both were regulars at the course and lived nearby. Kevin and Jeff guided me around the course which has several blind shots with small undulating greens. If you're not practiced at uphill/downhill/sidehill lies, this course will be tough. While we finished the last five holes in a light rain, these guys made it an enjoyable round.

We saw wildlife on the course, foxes, snakes and many birds. Unfortunately, I only captured a picture of the fox, as he was very happy to pose for us on the 6th tee.

The closing holes on this course are very good. Number 16 is a 420-yard par 4 that shares the fairway with #17, a 415-yard par 4 coming back the other way. It would require a massive 70-yard slice to impact play on either hole. Both holes have a carry over a barranca, Number 16 off the tee and number 17 on the approach. The 16th green is also guarded on the left by a deep bunker and on the right by a stand of trees. The 17th has a small bunker on the right, but a wide natural area in front of the green forcing a carry to the green. The 18th is a 500-yard dogleg left par 5 with a large natural area between the tee and the fairway; cut off as much as you can, get home in two and try to make an easy birdie.

My favorite hole on the course was the 500-yard 11th. It is very narrow with mounds on the right and heavy rough down the entire left side. The green is very small and guarded by two bunkers on the left with very deep rough. It can be a straightforward birdie, but also very easy to make a 7 or higher with one errant shot.

Approach Shots at Waverly Woods

Some Views at Waverly Woods

Massachusetts

Massachusetts is one of the most important states for golf in the United States. In 1913, Francis Ouimet, a 20-year-old American amateur, won the US Open at the Country Club in Brookline (just outside Boston) defeating seasoned British professionals Harry Vardon (winner in 1900) and Ted Ray (winner in 1920). Golf in the United States became cool.

The municipal courses in downtown Boston are typical muni's … with history. Both the William Devine and George Wright golf courses were designed by Donald Ross. The layouts are fun and interesting for even the best player. William J. Devine Golf Course at Franklin Park was established October 26, 1896 and is the second oldest public golf course in the United States behind Van Cortlandt Park in the Bronx borough of New York City. Historically, Willie Campbell was the first professional and Bobby Jones played here often.

The George Wright course was opened in 1938 after receiving President Roosevelt's Workers Progress Administration (WPA) funding to complete the construction. It has again gained notoriety by being chosen as Golf Digest's Best Municipal Course in Massachusetts and the 14th Best Municipal Golf Course in the U.S. by Golfweek in 2009.

We went there to celebrate our buddy, Tom Goodwin and his 50th birthday. Tom was the first base coach for the Red Sox at the time so we flew up to hang out with him, watch him work and play some golf. After the golf we caught a few Red Sox games at Fenway and sampled the nightlife around the stadium. It was an outstanding trip. We played William Devine, George Wright and Granite Links. Granite Links, just outside Boston in Quincy, MA quickly became my favorite course in the area.

Course: Granite Links

Type: Public

Website: https://www.granitelinks.com/

Location: Quincy, MA

Phone: 617-296-7600

Par 72. Yardage Played 6,379 (Blue)

Rating: 71.6/132

The Granite links clubhouse and pub was quintessential New England with excellent clam chowder and good food. The course itself has 27 holes. We played the Quincy/Milton Combination that I thoroughly enjoyed. The course presented excellent challenges off the tee and on the approach, but nothing that could not be handled by an 18 handicap or better, if they were playing from the appropriate tees.

The Granite Links site was originally a quarry and a landfill that was turned into an enjoyable 27 holes with brilliant skyline views and a lot of side hill lies. Granite links is not overly long, in fact, the longest hole is only 518 yards. The terrain and the wind combine to make the yardages somewhat mute. Almost every shot is up hill or downhill either with a helping or hurting wind. Thus, every shot seems to play significantly longer or shorter than the posted yardage.

At just 323 yards, the 7th on the Milton 9 is a fun hole with a 150-yard forced carry to a wide fairway with midline bunkers starting at 190 yards extending all the way to this shallow green. The ideal line is probably down the right with driver/3 wood, as there is not much space short or left to lay-up. The 7th on the Granite 9 is a stunning 218-yard par 3 with a great view of the landscape.

I liked the course and would go back again unless I could get on The Country Club in Brookline.

Views from Granite Links

The Guys Enjoying our Trip to Boston

Michigan

Michigan is known for a lot of things. Henry Ford and Detroit automobile manufacturing. MoTown music and the amazing artists. Cherries! The largest football stadium in the United States. Michigan is known as "The Great Lake State." The Great Lakes touch 8 states – but Michigan is the only state that touches four of the five lakes, with borders on Superior, Michigan, Huron and Erie. Michigan only misses Ontario. It has 3,200 miles of shoreline.

The 45th parallel runs through Michigan. This line of latitude cuts through the state near Traverse City ("Cherry Capital of the World"), making it the ½ waypoint between the Equator and the North Pole. This has two effects on Michigan Golf:

1. it makes the season short, generally mid-May to Halloween.
2. it provides 18 hours per day of sunlight during the summer making the emergency 18 almost a requirement.

Michigan has 650 public golf courses along with more than 100 private courses. We decided to do a buddy's trip one September. Our trip included three wonderful resorts: Arcadia Bluffs, Forest Dunes, Manistee National and a daily fee gem, The Links at Bowen Lake, near Grand Rapids.

Course: Arcadia Bluffs - Bluffs
Type: Resort
Website: https://arcadiabluffs.com
Location: Arcadia, MI
Phone: (800) 494-8666
Par 72. Yardage Played 6,389 (White)
Rating: 70.5/134

Arcadia Bluffs is truly stunning. Warren Henderson designed a links course that sits on the edge of Lake Michigan with amazing views. The wind speed and direction control club selection requiring strategic decisions at every turn. It is a great course deserving of its ranking as one of the best courses in the United States. A couple of fun things about Arcadia Bluffs were the flagsticks being only five feet tall (instead of the traditional 7) and shaped differently, not a triangle or rectangle, but more of a parallelogram. Sitting in the Adirondack Chairs after the round with a glass of Scotch and watching other players approach the 18th is pretty close to heaven.

Views from Arcadia Bluffs

Before visiting Arcadia Bluffs we spent two days at the Forest Dunes Resort. We played both Forest Dunes and The Loop Course. The entrance to the property is marked by a simple sign with a deer logo and guests enjoy the 15,000 square foot clubhouse that includes a formal and private dining room, well stocked pro shop, various meeting spaces plus beautifully appointed locker rooms with showers for both men and women. We stayed in a room on property about 30 yards from the clubhouse.

The Forest Dunes course was designed by Tom Weiskopf with a lot of Risk/Reward shots for you to consider. It is ranked higher than The Loop by many publications. The wild Turkeys roaming the course was fun. The front nine had variety of trees with strong bunkering while the second nine has a lot of native areas with scruffy underbrush and sandy waste areas. My favorite hole was the short par 4 17th. Playing only 278 yards for us, it turned out to be a beast for several in our group. It is an outstanding parkland layout. The course also includes a 19th hole, 130 yards over water to help you settle any bets that couldn't be decided by the 18th.

Course: Forest Dunes

Type: Resort

Website: https://www.forestdunesgolf.com

Location: Roscommon, MI

Phone: (989) 275.0700

Par 72. Yardage Played 6,309 (II/III Combo)

Rating: 71.3/135

Views at Forest Dunes

My favorite course on this adventure, however, was "The Loop" at Forest Dunes. A Tom Doak design, The Loop, is eighteen green complexes that can be played either clockwise ("Red") or counterclockwise ("Black"). For example, Red 4 is a 180-yard par-3 that plays uphill into the southwest corner of the property. Its green enjoys many Redan characteristics as the land tilts from right to left. It's a very fine hole that would be a welcome addition on most courses. Its 'cousin,' the 480-yard Black 14 par 5 approaches the Red Redan green from 90 degrees, meaning that the Black 14 putting surface tilts from back to front toward the golfer in the fairway.

Course: The Loop - Red
Type: Resort
Website: https://www.forestdunesgolf.com
Location: Roscommon, MI
Phone: (989) 275.0700
Par 70. Yardage Played 6,064 (Middle)
Rating: 68.7/117

We played the Red routing on this visit. The red routing is currently ranked as the 12th best course in Michigan and has been as high as #47 in the 100 greatest public courses in the United States. I will go back to play the Black routing as soon as possible. Given everywhere I have played, there is nothing quite like The Loop. It is sort of a cross of Old MacDonald at Bandon Dunes with touches of the Old Course at Saint Andrews. There are wide fairways, hidden bunkers, funny bounces and long rolls.

The starter gave us two rules for playing the course.

(1) Do not drive the cart over the tee marker. All of the grass at The Loop was the same, Tee boxes, fairways and greens. They were just mowed to different heights and a single "Tee Flag" was placed in the grass. You just drove right up to it, decided which side you wanted to tee from and hit it!

(2) Do not drink so much so that you drive into fairway bunkers on the course. Some bunkers were "hidden" in that you could only see the top but the bunker was on the other side. It was possible to drive over the top and into a bunker if you weren't paying attention.

Driving up to the tee marker and teeing off at The Loop

The course plays firm and fast, requiring shots that hit well short of the greens to roll to the target. The ground game is king here. When your approach shot lands on the green it sounds like a drum, and without tour level height and spin, the ball bounds into bunkers, tall grasses, or deep swales. Most holes offer numerous ways to play off the tee to set up angles into the greens, and while some tee shots appear narrow, there is surprising width available. There are few green side bunkers or elevated greens so the primary challenge is on and around the greens, which can sometime be a bit unplayable for recovery shots.

This course is quite gentle off the tee – the fairways are wide and don't tilt toward hazards or deep rough – but be careful of the swales, mounds and "backwards hazards." The swales and mounds can move your ball 30 to 50 yards in an unexpected direction. Furthermore, there are a couple spots where a bunker is angled such that it's visible on the Black routing but nearly invisible on the Red Routing, or vice versa. It's hard to miss a fairway, so, the course is really defined by the greens, which are very firm, large, multi-tiered and very fast. Most golfers will find the fairway and can take advantage of some of the shorter holes as long as their short game holds up. The greens are huge but difficult to get close to the flag because of double, even triple breaks and navigating large swales. There are no double greens at The Loop. Because the course is played only in one direction each day, there are eighteen greens to go with the eighteen holes.

My favorite hole at the Loop was the finishing par 4 eighteenth. We played it at slightly over 400, it demands a shot down the middle into a valley followed by a blind shot back up to the green.

The yardages change daily at the Bootlegger, our gang on the 10th green

Views of The Loop

The bunker rakes are made of wood that match the character of the course and leave furrows in the sand rather than making them completely smooth. If you want to see how firm, fast, reversible golf courses can play, make a plan to head to The Loop at Forest Dunes.

The resort also has a 10-hole par 3 course called "The Bootlegger" and an outstanding putting green with 18 challenging holes for a little late afternoon, evening wagering.

We also played a daily fee course near Grand Rapids called The Links at Bowen Lake. This was a tight, tree-lined course that was a bargain at $40. One of the coolest golf sculptures I have seen was in front of the clubhouse and Restaurant.

Golfing Family in Front of The Links at Bowen Lake

Minnesota

I have spent some time in Minnesota, working with clients in the Twin Cities and then dating a lady whose family was from there. I had never played golf in Minnesota. There are amazing courses in Minnesota including Interlachen, Minikahda, Hazeltine and Somerset to name a few.

We did not play those …

During COVID, my good friend, Kevin and I were driving from Texas to play in a tournament at Sand Valley and Mammoth Dunes in Wisconsin. We decided to stop in Rochester Minnesota to sample the local course. Rochester Country Club, an AW Tillinghast design being restored by Tom Doak, is consistently rated as one of the best courses in the state.

We didn't play there, either.

We chose Maple Valley Golf and Country Club for no particular reason other than it was relatively close to the road we were traveling on. Maple Valley was designed by Wayne Idso. As we arrived and went into the pro shop, I was noticing that they sold hats with netting on them to cover your face. I jokingly asked Kevin if we needed to buy hats with nets, he told me "No, we're good."

He was wrong!

After teeing off on the first hole and driving about 200 yards we were swarmed with gnats and mosquitos! It was difficult to open your eyes and do not, under any circumstances open your mouth. Keeping them out of your ears was menacing!

Maple Valley has limestone bluffs and the Root River bordering it on three sides giving it natural boundaries and difficulty. The first hole was a short, downhill par 4 with a steep drop at about 240 yards off the tee to a tiny green that ran away from you. It was hard to see with all the bugs, the hat with a net would have been a bargain.

Course: Maple Valley

Type: Public

Website:

https://www.maplevalleygolf.com

Location: Rochester, MN

Phone: 507-285-9100

Par 71. Yardage Played 6,270

(Blue)

Rating: 70.5/121

The second hole was a short par 5 that started down in the valley below the clubhouse but climbed back up the hill to a nice vista. While on the tee box, however, the gnats did not let up. We were already exhausted by the time we got to number three, a stunning 160-yard par 3 with a 50 foot drop in elevation. The wind can really play tricks here. From that point on, the course was very scenic and a fun round.

Several holes use the river that runs through the course, and it has been identified as a "Hidden Gem" by Minnesota Golfer Magazine and named as a "places to play" by Golf Digest. The back-to-back par 5's, numbers 14 and 15, make for a very scorable stretch and overall, the course is very playable once you get past the gnats and mosquitos.

Some views of Maple Valley

Maple Valley Views

Mississippi

Otherwise known as the Magnolia State, Mississippi is one of the southern states in the US and a big part of the idea of "southern hospitality." Elvis Presley, Brittany Spears and the "Black Swan", Elizabeth Taylor Greenfield were all born in Mississippi making it a major contributor to the US music scene. The golf scene is not as prestigious, but the 140 golf courses in the state offer a variety of playing styles.

Dancing Rabbit Golf Club commemorates one of the most popular assembly grounds on the Choctaw Indian tribal lands. It is named for its location on the banks of the Big and Little Dancing Rabbit Creeks. In the Choctaw language it is BOK CHUKFI AHITHAC, "the creek where rabbits dance." It was like a well-tended park–beautiful, spacious–beneath a canopy of mature trees. This area was transformed into two good golf courses: The Azaleas and The Oaks.

Course: Dancing Rabbit
Type: Resort
Website:
https://dancingrabbitgolf.com
Location: Philadelphia, MS
Phone: (601) 663-0011
Azaleas Par 72. Yardage Played 7,158 (Gold)
Rating: 74.4/135
Oaks Par 72. Yardage Played 7,076 (Gold)   Rating 74.6/139

Opened in 1997 and renovated in 2016, The Tom Fazio designed, Azaleas course has Bermuda tees and fairways and Tif Eagle greens. The Azaleas course has received numerous awards and accolades including spots on Golf Magazine's Top 100 You Can Play list and Golf & Travel's Top 100 Modern Courses, as well as Golf Digest's Top 10 New Upscale Public Golf Courses ranking. It has hosted a LPGA event.

The Oaks golf course was opened in 1999 and is as equally charming and challenging as The Azaleas. The Oaks has well maintained Tif Bermuda greens and Zoysia fairways. The Zoysia fairways are wonderful and provide a nearly perfect lie for every shot, this is an excellent combination southern courses offer that provides an exceptional experience for the golfer.

The clubhouse is a three-story plantation home with high ceilings and two wrap around verandas. It is very comfortable and spacious. One of the guys in our group said "I could live here." Golf, Gambling, and Southern Charm, what's not to love?

It rained heavily in the days leading up to our visit and the courses were cart path only making for long walks and a lot of three wood practice into the par 4s. The courses played very long. Wherever the ball hit the ground off the tee was where it stopped, often plugged. I personally preferred the Oaks course under our conditions because the Zoysia grass helped the fairways drain better and the ball was easier to hit. The casino was a good diversion and the restaurants inside were decent.

Most of the par 3 holes were downhill and very manageable. The 571-yard par 5 fifth on the Azaleas and the 577-yard 9th on the Oaks were beasts in the wet weather that we encountered, the rest of the par 5s were in the 500-530 range and very playable. Both courses had excellent variation in the par 4s, short ones in the 320-yard range and long ones in the 460-yard ones. The key was the uphill or downhill slopes that made them.

We had a group of sixteen golfers from multiple courses in the Austin area for this trip. It was a fun time, and I would recommend Dancing Rabbit for a buddy's trip if you're in the area.

Scenes from Dancing Rabbit

The Hills at Dancing Rabbit

Tough shots at Dancing Rabbit

Missouri

Missouri is "The Show Me State." It is tied with Tennessee for bordering the most states. The eight states Missouri borders are Arkansas, Illinois, Kansas, Iowa, Nebraska, Oklahoma, Tennessee and Kentucky. Missouri is known for its random oversized objects.; for example, there is a 12-foot-long pecan, a giant rocking chair that's more than 42 feet tall, a 43-foot-tall rooster and the world's largest chess piece — 53 times as big as a regular-size piece. The St. Louis Arch is very cool and the Budweiser Brewery with the magnificent Clydesdales are a fun visit.

Missouri is home to some amazing golf courses. From Kansas City to St. Louis or from Kirksville to Branson. There are more than 400 courses in the state. The Branson area has Payne's Valley at Big Cedar Lodge and in St. Louis, the Hale Irwin-designed Quail Creek Golf Club is a Par-72 course that will challenge novice and veteran golfers alike. Personally, my favorite course was at Porto Cima. The golf course features five sets of tees, generous landing areas and seven holes that play beside or over the Lake. It's a wonderful experience for all levels of player and recently, Golf Digest recognized The Club at Porto Cima as one of the best private golf courses in America. It is a Jack Nicklaus signature design that has hosted several state championships. Unfortunately, I have no pictures of my round at this wonderful Ozarks location.

Course: Old Hawthorne
Type: Daily Fee
Website:
https://www.oldhawthorne.com/
Location: Columbia, MO
Phone: 573-442-5280
Par 72.   Yardage Played 6,234 (Middle)
Rating: 70.3/126

Another good course that I played is Old Hawthorne in Columbia, Mo. Designed by award-winning golf architect Art Schaupeter, the course has five sets of tees. It opened in 2007 and is the home course for the University of Missouri golf team. It is very modern, regardless of the name. The original portion of the clubhouse was built in 1938 as an exact replica of President Andrew

Jackson's home, "The Hermitage." The interior has been remodeled, increasing its space from 6,000 to 30,000 square feet, with many of the original hardwood floors buffed to a new gleam.

Scenes from Old Hawthorne Clubhouse and First Tee

The golf course plays over rolling terrain with multiple water hazards. All the tee boxes are mowed as squares giving the course an "old style" feel. The fairways are extremely wide, with six of them having center fairway bunkers that split the fairways, creating many different options of how to attack the green. The course is designed with several "Redan" greens. That is, the green slopes from front to back, and is angled from front right to back left. It usually has the entrance to the green kept open, allowing shots to roll onto the putting surface, and the left flank of the green has bunkering beside it.

I played with my friend and colleague Dan Yates and it is him that we have to thank for the pictures of the course.

The 5th hole is a personal favorite. It is a 360-yard dogleg left par 4 with water down the left side. Cut off as much as you want to shorten your approach. Since it is a relatively short hole, the safe play is to hit the tee shot right and stuff a short iron or wedge close.

The 10th hole, a 510-yard par-5 requires a precise tee shot down the left side between a pair of massive Oak trees from an elevated tee. With water down the right side and Grindstone creek in front of the green, the second shot demands serious attention. The green is reachable in two but the orientation of the green and the contours within the surface require a player to hit a precise shot if they expect to have any hope of eagle or birdie.

The 18th is an excellent finishing hole, dubbed "Oak Hill,". Number 18 is a 380-yard par 4 with 10 bunkers dotting the fairway and a pond to your right off the tee. This hole continues with the theme of choosing a line off the tee, left is very wide and safe, but leaves a longer and somewhat blind approach. Right is shorter and narrower, additionally the bunkers are vicious. The green is huge and has a lot of undulation meaning it is an easy three putt if your approach is not in the right area.

The view of the 5th Hole at Old Hawthorne

Montana

Montana, Big Sky Country, miles and miles of beautiful landscapes and small towns. The movie *A River Runs Through It* and the TV Series *Yellowstone* have brought the beauty of Montana to millions of people. Billings is the largest city in Montana and the seat of Yellowstone County. It has a population of around 120,000 people for 10 golf courses. We were lucky that our friend, Bobby Collier, introduced us to a member at Yellowstone Country Club, a very nice private course in the area.

Yellowstone Country Club is a private 7,100-yard course designed by Robert Trent Jones, Sr in 1958 with an update by Carl Thuesen in 2007. It is a stunning parkland course with a lot of mature trees and deep rough that requires precise shot making to score well.

Course: Yellowstone CC
Type: Private
Website:
https://www.yellowstonecc.com
Location: Billings, MT
Phone: (406) 656-1701
Par 72. Yardage Played 6,462
(Member)
Rating: 71.0/129

Like most Robert Trent Jones courses, Yellowstone Country Club is heavily bunkered. It also has a lot of mature trees that define your hitting areas. There are also a lot of dogleg holes on this course. My favorite hole was the 2nd. A 380-yard dogleg left with a bunker guarding the bend. Once that is negotiated, there is a stream running in front of the green, don't be short. The bunkers on the left and right of the green are also to be considered. Basically, this hole demands straight and precise… the theme of the day.

Scenes from Yellowstone Country Club

Another course we played in Montana was near the town of Emigrant on the Mountain Sky Guest Ranch. Named after a nearby peak along the Yellowstone River, it is a scenic location with panoramic vistas, geysers and waterfalls. The course was called Rising Sun, and it is part of the Mountain Sky Guest Ranch. In addition to the 18-hole layout, Rising Sun also has a fun par 3 course! An upscale dude ranch resort, Mountain Sky has many activities available, including horseback riding, ATV and fishing. The golf course, Rising Sun, is the only Johnny Miller designed course I have played, and it was amazing. Stunning vistas, excellent shot values with elevation changes and greens that were undulating, but fun to putt on. Through our conservation efforts, Rising Sun Golf Course is the first golf course in Montana to become a certified Audubon Cooperative Sanctuary by Audubon International. Made me wish Johnny Miller had designed more than 17 courses, I plan to try a few more. Here's a recommended list I was sent by his design firm.

CALIFORNIA

- Maderas Golf Club
- Whitney Oaks
- Schaffers Mill
- Brighton Crest Golf &CC
- Eagle Ridge Golf Club
- Stonetree Golf Club
- Silverado Resort (north course redesign)

NEVADA

- Genoa Lakes Golf Resort Golf Course

FLORIDA

- Harmony Golf Preserve

UTAH

- Thanksgiving Point
- Entrada At Snow Canyon

NEW JERSEY

- Due Process Stable Golf Club

Course: Rising Sun
Type: Resort
Website:
https://www.mountainsky.com/
Location: Emigrant, MT
Phone: 1-800-548-3392
Par 72. Yardage Played 6,656 (Blue)
Rating: 69.8/125

The head PGA professional at Rising Sun, Matt Bader, played with us along with an assistant, Colby George. Matt is in the cowboy hat (it is a dude ranch, after all) and Colby is in the sunglasses. Colby took the money that day with an Eagle on 18! It was fun to watch. 90% of Golf is who you play with…

The Group at Rising Sun Golf Course

This was a stunning course with views of the Absaroka and Gallatin mountains on all sides of a fantastic meadow in Paradise Valley. The sloping terrain and elevation made it feel like the ball flew forever. The par 3s were a nice two downhill and two slightly uphill. The greens were fantastic although Matt mentioned they sometimes have a problem with the Elk walking through them. My favorite hole was the 18th. A downhill, double dogleg, 530-yard par 5 with a sloping green. The view from the tee was incredible with a clear target in the distance.

The 18th at Rising Sun from the Tee

Scenes from Rising Sun

Nebraska

Nebraska means "Flat Water" and that pretty much describes the cornhusker state. It used to be called the "Great American Desert" but has large underground water reserves and may have more miles of rivers than any other US State. The sand hills take up 25% of the state and up to one million sand hill cranes fly through every year. The soil in Nebraska is designed for golf courses. In fact, the soil sample sent to the USGA for the Sand Hills CC, in Mullen NE, was exactly the chemistry recommended by the USGA. It is amazing how many outstanding courses there are in the Cornhusker state. There are more than 200 courses in Nebraska with Sand Hills heading the list. A couple of other destinations, The Prairie Club in Valentine, Dismal River in Mullen, and Wild Horse in Gothenburg are highly rated and offer spectacular golf. Sand Hills is an incredible course in the west part of Nebraska. It was a five and one-half hour drive from Omaha across a time zone. It's shorter to fly into Denver, CO and drive to Mullen, but we wanted to see the College World Series first.

Sand Hills is very private. A google search will find a lot of reviews and recommendations on the course, but they do not have their own website. We were lucky enough to get on Sand Hills through our friend Bill Moretti, a Golf Digest Top 50 Instructor in the United States and a Texas Golf Hall of Fame inductee. One of the most genuine guys on the planet, Bill teaches out of Austin Golf Club in Spicewood, Texas and helped us to write a letter to the Chairman of Sand Hills to get a coveted tee time at this TOP 10 in the world golf course (according to Golf Magazine, https://golf.com/travel/courses/top-100-courses-world-ranking-2021-2022).

Course: Sand Hills
Type: Private
Website:
Location: Mullen, NE
Phone: (308) 546-2437
Par 71. Yardage Played 6,434
Rating: None

The 19th hole, known as "Ben's Porch," had burgers and brats fresh off the grill along with plenty of beverages available. It has a spectacular vibe and gives golfers a chance to relax and hang out. We met several new friends before and after our round on Ben's Porch.

Sand Hills Golf Club

The course itself is wide open with clear views. Our caddies took us around with excellent instruction on where to hit the shot, not that we were able to execute, but the intent was wonderful. The first hole is a dogleg left par 5 from an elevated tee that overlooks the Nebraska plains. It is fun! The greens are large and undulating (Ben Crenshaw at his best), the course has a tremendous amount of sand in gigantic bunkers on both sides of the fairway and surrounding several greens. Because of the course design, changing winds and weather, along with many possible pin placements, there is no course rating or slope at Sand Hills, every day is different. The greens were very fast, the fairways were firm and the tee-boxes smooth. It was everything you would expect from a top tier private course. Between the design and the conditions, you could use a variety of shot styles to get the job done.

It wasn't pure links, but many elements of links golf were in play. I really liked the finishing stretch of holes 16, 17 and 18. Hole #16 is the longest par 5 on the course at 612 yards. It has a huge fairway with a blowout bunker on the left side that simply must be avoided for any chance to make par. The tee shot is downhill while the rest of the hole is uphill as it plays mostly straight with a tilt left for the second half of the hole. The 17th hole is the perfect example of a tough short par 3. It plays only 150 yards from the back tee, but the saddle nature of the green with danger for just about any miss makes this a real shot makers hole. The final hole is both a brute and a beauty as it plays long and uphill. It has a very picturesque windmill just off the left side of the fairway. If you ever get a chance, play this course.

Walking with Caddies at Sand Hills Golf Club

Wide-open spaces at Sand Hills Golf Club

Nevada

Nevada is nicknamed "The Silver State" because America's Largest Silver Deposit, the Comstock Lode, was discovered there in 1859. It is also the largest Gold producing state in the United States. While other states have casinos, Nevada is the undisputed King of Gambling in the United States. In Billy Walter's book <u>Gambler,</u> he talks about gambling and golfing in Las Vegas. There are only 88 golf courses in Nevada, with more than 50 of those in the Las Vegas area. The mountain layouts in the Reno/Lake Tahoe are wonderful, but it is the desert gems in the Las Vegas region that most people have played. I have played only 16 courses in Las Vegas, including the three at the Paiute Resort and the two TPC courses, Las Vegas and Summerlin. It is always fun to watch the PGA tour guys play Summerlin and realize how far they hit it and how good they are after playing there. Watching Bryson DeChambeau drive a par 4 green that requires me to hit a good drive and a solid wedge is truly amazing. Furthermore, the line he takes is unbelievable over the trees that are not even in my field of view.

I have never played Shadow Creek, but it is consistently ranked as the best course in the region. George Archer told me it was his favorite course in the United States. Bali Hai is fun, close to the strip and airport and consistently in great condition. The Paiute courses, Coyote Canyon, Reflection Bay, and Canyon Gate CC are all enjoyable.

In Vegas, where replication is king, two of the city's finest efforts are not in plush hotels and casinos, but on the golf course. Bear's Best and Royal Links pay tribute to Jack Nicklaus and to The Open Championship. Bear's Best replicates 18 of Jack's favorite holes from his courses, some with the black sand that is fun to play from. Royal Links Golf Club was a personal favorite. It gave the golfer a realistic feel of the famous British Isle links courses, sadly, Royal Links closed in 2021.

Course: Dragon Ridge
Type: Private
Website: https://dragonridge.com/
Location: Las Vegas, NV
Phone: (702) 614-4444
Par 72. Yardage Played 6,413
Rating: 71.6/138

Dragon Ridge is a relative newcomer to the Las Vegas scene. Named after a rocky ridge known to residents as the "Sleeping Dragon" the Jay Morrish and Dave Druzidky design opened in 2001. The course has received a bevy of accolades including Best Golf Course in Las Vegas for 2020 and 2021. Top 10 best course in Nevada by Golf Digest and Top Private course in Southern Nevada by Review Journals. It is that good.

Dragon Ridge features sweeping elevation changes, natural canyons and rock formations. It has generous fairways and landing areas. The forced carries over desert are reasonable, but not a pushover. Water comes into play on just three holes. Every hole offers a bail out alternative, so strategic choices abound. In total, it is an environment that provides a great deal of variety in shot selection.

The par three holes offer incredible views of the Las Vegas Strip and the Sloan Canyon Conservation area. The conditioning from tee to green rivals that of any course I have played. Most golfers will have the opportunity to hit every club in their bag, and everyone should enjoy the natural desert mountain environment.

This course plays tougher than the yardage and rating suggest. The wind and the elevation changes are strong. The rough is sticky and punishing and playing an approach from the desert is nearly impossible. The fairways are lush and the greens are smooth, notice where you are on the mountain to understand the break.

Views at Dragon Ridge Country Club

The first six holes are straightforward and lull you into a sense of security. Only the second, a downhill 200-yard par 3 is a difficult par in the early third. Holes seven through fifteen require strategy and precision on the meat of the course. The elevated green on the long par 4 7th can cause grief after avoiding the lake down the right side and the waterfall near the putting surface. Holes 9 and 11 are longer uphill par 4s that require an extra club. The final three holes allow for an exciting finish. Sixteen is a short par 4 of 290 yards. Seventeen is a gettable 160-yard par 3 and eighteen played 520 yards par 5 for our round. All three provide birdie opportunities, but an errant shot and triple is in play.

Some Challenging Shots at Dragon Ridge

Dragon Ridge is a private course that is an absolute treat, if you ever get a chance to play there, you should do it!

New Hampshire

New Hampshire is known as the Granite State and its motto is one of the more famous for the United States, "Live Free or Die." New Hampshire is not known for its golf. There are only about 100 courses in the state. My friends and I decided to tee it up at Breakfast Hill Golf Club in Greenland, NH. The championship par 71 layout has been ranked (since 2005) a top five course by Golf Week magazine as one of America's best daily fee facilities. In 2008 and 2009, 2018 Golf Digest awarded Breakfast Hill four stars as one of their "Best Places to Play". For countless seasons, the club has been recognized as a top public course by Golf Magazine and Golf.com.

Our experience wasn't that good. The course condition was ok, but not what we expected for late August and the accolades that we had seen. The course is short, roughly 6,400 from the tips and 5,800 from one set up. The fairways were narrow and the greens small, which is fine with such a short track, but it did reduce shot options and forced several layup shots.

Course: Breakfast Hill
Type: Public
Website:
https://www.breakfasthill.com
Location: Greenland, NH
Phone: (603) 436-5001
Par 71. Yardage Played 6,493
Rating: 71.5/130

The greens were bumpy and not in the best shape. The granite rock outcroppings on the edges of the fairways and the water hazards were well placed to protect the course from longer hitters. My favorite hole was the 8th. It is a short dogleg left par 4. Hit the tee shot down the right and it plays easy. Going left is likely in the creek or worse. The green is protected by a bunker on the right and there is trouble long.

Breakfast Hill
Golf Club
8
Cutts
Alley
Par
4
356
332
310
287

New Jersey

New Jersey is the Rodney Dangerfield of US states. It gets no respect. Jokes about the Garden State abound in movies and hardly anyone west of the Mississippi can name the capital (Trenton). In fact, it has the number one ranked course in the world in Clementon, NJ. Pine Valley. I have watched the Shell's Wonderful World of Golf with Byron Nelson and Gene Littler many times. A couple of my friends have played there. I have not. My rounds in New Jersey were at Cherry Valley Country Club in Skillman and Rock Spring Golf Club in West Orange. Rock Spring is one of two public courses in the US designed by legendary course architect Seth Raynor. Rock Spring is a relatively short course only 15 miles from Manhattan with interesting green complexes.

Course: Cherry Valley
Type: Private
Website:
https://www.invitedclubs.com/clubs/cherry-valley-country-club
Location: Skillman, NJ
Phone: (609) 466-4244
Par 72. Yardage Played 6,535 (white)
Rating: 71.6/133

Cherry Valley is an 18-hole Rees Jones designed golf course with large, undulated greens, contoured fairways, and was in pristine condition for the round I played. It was a Club Corp facility (now Invited) meaning that I had reciprocal privileges through my home course in Texas. Cherry Valley offered a nice combination of challenge and enjoyment. I found several opportunities to take some risks and experience the reward of a great shot. I was paired with two members, lawyers that worked in New York, that hit the ball a long way, but rarely where they needed it to go.

During the official grand opening of the golf course in 1991, DKM Properties presented Rees Jones, who attended, with a cast iron plaque signifying CVCC as his "Longest Course," not in yards, but in time spent on design!

The 177-yard par 3, 11th is the signature hole. It is named "Rees' Surprise," and features an elevated green with two large kidney-shaped bunkers on both sides. The sycamore on the left side is the basis for the course logo.

View across the bridge at CVCC

Approach Shots at Cherry Valley

149

Sycamore Tree used as the Logo for CVCC

New Mexico

New Mexico has very good golf. The best public courses include Cochiti, Paa-Ko Ridge, and Pinon Hills. All are worthy of your time and money. The Inn of the Mountain Gods in Ruidosa is fun and the University of New Mexico South course in Albuquerque is a good test. I have played all of these and a few more. I have not played Black Mesa but it gets rave reviews from those that have played it. My heart lies with the smaller municipal courses, though, like New Mexico Military Institute (NMMI) course where Nancy Lopez used to play and Jal Country Club, home of Kathy Whitworth.

LPGA Hall of Famer Kathy Whitworth has won more professional tour victories than any other golfer on either the LPGA or PGA Tours. Growing up on a 9 hole course in Jal, New Mexico, Whitworth captured the New Mexico State Women's Amateur in 1957 and 1958. She made her way to Texas and the Whitworth Course at Trophy Club is fantastic. Here is a look at the first tee there commemorating her 88 tour wins.

Nancy Lopez grew up in Roswell, NM and now the old Springhill course (home of the Chiconky Open, a two-person better ball event in which one Chicano player is paired with a Honky player via blind draw) is named after her.

Course: Spring River
Type: Public
Website: https://roswell-nm.gov/226/Golf-Course
Location: Roswell, NM
Phone: (575) 622-9506
Par 71. Yardage Played 6,623 (Blue)
Rating: 69.9/124

Nancy won the New Mexico Women's Amateur at age 12 in 1969, and the U.S. Girls' Junior at 15! During her first full season on the LPGA Tour in 1978, Nancy won five consecutive events and nine overall! She won another eight times in 1979 and won multiple times in each year from 1980 to 1984. New Mexico has provided the world with great golfers!

I have played Spring River many times as my mother-in-law lived across the street from the 15th green for several years. It is a fun track that is very walkable. The 15th hole is a 495-yard par 5 with a pond on the left side of the green. The approach shot requires precision to get a birdie.

Neither Kathy Whitworth nor Nancy Lopez honed their games on lush green country club fairways or smooth quick greens. To experience the game the way they grew up, travel to Santa Rosa, New Mexico and play the nine-hole municipal course there. At the intersection of I-40 and Route 85 on the Pecos River, Santa Rosa is a good place for a sportsman with the Reservoir managed by the Corps of Engineers and the Blue Hole for Scuba Diving. Yes, Scuba Diving in New Mexico! Golf is not a strong point in Santa Rosa, however. The course is nine holes, about 3100 yards, and not lush. The wind provides a strong defense. The tee boxes and greens were well manicured and in fabulous condition. There were no fairways to speak of, in fact, when my brother and I played, we had hitting mats attached to our cart to place the ball upon for approach shots so as not to damage our clubs on the rocks. We had a wonderful time. I thoroughly enjoy playing with my brother, 90% of golf is who you play with.

Course: Tres Lagunas
Type: Public
Website:
https://www.santarosabluehole.com/tres-lagunas-golf-course/
Location: Santa Rosa, NM
Phone: (575) 472-4653
Par 36. Yardage Played 3,158
Rating: 73.1/123

Santa Rosa Municipal Golf course from Google Maps

New York

New York is a big state, both in square miles and attitude. The 27th ranked state by size holds the United States' most populous city with about 8.5 million people. Obviously "The City" is a populated concrete jungle, however "upstate" is beautiful with trees, mountains, and water. There are more than 875 golf courses in the Empire State. Some of them are awesome, but I believe there is a strong Northeast bias in golf course rankings. Fourteen of the Golf Digest Top 50 courses in the US are in New York State, most in the "metropolis" area. I am sorry, but I am not buying it. Personally, I have played Bethpage Black and Piping Rock. Both fine golf courses, but certainly not in my ranking of the top 50 in the United States.

In 1940, Sam Snead declared Bethpage Black to be an unfair test of golf. It has been redesigned several times since then. In fact, two plaques pay tribute to the course architects, A.W. Tillinghast and Rees Jones near the practice green.

Tribute Plaques to the Course Architects

I enjoyed Bethpage Black immensely. I flew into NY on a Sunday morning and drove over to the park on my way to Somers for business meetings the next week. I walked up to the counter and asked about availability and the lady said we can have you out in 30 minutes with another single! I teed off at 1 pm playing with a young man on the Yale golf team. He played the blue tees (about 7,400 yards), I played the white tees (6,700 yards). We had a wonderful round together talking about school, work, and golf. The caddie statue that greets you and represents the logo are excellent reminders of the day.

Course: Bethpage - Black
Type: Public
Website:
https://www.bethpagegolfcourse.com
Location: Farmingdale, NY
Phone: (516) 249-4040
Par 71. Yardage Played 6,684 (White)
Rating: 74.0/145

Expecting to shoot 90 after flying, driving and not hitting balls prior to the round, I played great with a 78! The course has a lot of elevated greens with heavy bunkering and thick, heavy rough. The greens are a mixture of bent and poa annua grass making them slick to putt, but sticky on chips at the same time… it was a bit strange.

Like St. Andrews, be prepared for an audience on the opening tee box, as other golfers and spectators mull on the patio as you hit. The 1st hole at the Bethpage Black is a 429-yard sharp dogleg right. It is a good opening hole that eases you into the round. The drive from this elevated tee box is a fun one. The goal is to reach the dogleg, which requires a solid 260-yard poke. Anything short of this might be blocked out by thick trees that line the entire right side.

In general, the tee shots on the Black Course are not difficult, the landing areas are fairly wide but with the doglegs, the bunkers, and the undulations hitting the ball to the right spot in the fairway to have a decent approach is not easy. The scorecard says the 13th hole is a 480-yard par 5 from the Whites but on the day I played, the tees were moved back closer to the 554 yards, where it played in the Open.

The tee shot and second shot on the 13th is the narrowest on the course, with dense woods lining the entire length of this tight fairway. This hole is also extremely well-bunkered on the left side with sand between 150 to 200 yards from the tee and about 140 yards short of the green. It is a tough par 5.

Tee Shots at Bethpage Black

The back nine has two phenomenal par 3 holes. The 14th and the 17th both require solid shots to make par and a birdic is a bonus. The 14th plays at 150 yards and the 17th at 195 yards. The 17th hole plays uphill to an exceedingly shallow putting surface. Pretty much all you can see from the tee box are five bunkers ready to swallow your ball on all sides of the green.

Par 3 14th Hole at Bethpage Black

Number 17 at Bethpage Black

North Carolina

North Carolina is a fantastic state … the beaches, the mountains, the sand belt. The Raleigh area is a beacon of medical and high-tech innovation. Blue Devils-Tar Heels-Wolfpack ... wonderful basketball and fantastic educators. Fine golf can be found in all parts of the state. Bear Lake Reserve in the western mountains of North Carolina is stunning in the fall and the Nicklaus Course there is one of his most fun designs. My friend, John, plays there regularly and sends wonderful pictures of bears, deer and beautifully manicured greens.

Bears playing on the cart path between #7 and #8 at Bear Lake Reserve

Oyster Bay on Sunset Beach in the southeast part of the state is a good test. In the early 1980s it was voted resort course of the year. As recently as 2009 it was heralded as one of the best public courses in America. Be careful of the gators though, there are some huge ones on this course!

The most famous course in North Carolina is probably Pinehurst #2 in the sand belt. The Pinehurst resort is about 71 miles from Raleigh and 83 miles from Greensboro airports. Pinehurst's founder, James Walker Tufts, made his fortune selling silverware and soda pop! He wanted Pinehurst to be a health resort for people of modest means. It became the epicenter for American golf. He hired Donald Ross to oversee the day-to-day operations. Ross was a Scottish-born immigrant who trained as a young man with Old Tom Morris at St. Andrews in the 1890s. He then spent most of his career and life in America, where he designed many of the world's championship courses amid the "Golden Age of Golf." Ross specifically built dozens of iconic fairways throughout the country, including Aronimink Golf Club, Seminole Golf Club, and the Oak Hill Country Club. His influence on the game continues to this day. In fact, there are more than fifty Donald Ross courses in North Carolina, which means around 10% of the state's 600 golf courses (Scotland has a similar number of courses) were touched by the prolific Scotsman.

Course: Pinehurst - #2
Type: Resort
Website:
http://www.pinehurst.com
Location: Pinehurst, NC
Phone: (855) 235-8507
Par 72. Yardage Played 6,752 (Blue)
Rating: 72.8/131

Some friends and I went to Pinehurst in 2005 to play in a Pro-Am on four courses, #2, #4, #6, and #8. We also played #7 for fun. What a fantastic trip! Besides the golf, it was memorable walking through the Carolina Hotel and sitting in the rockers on the deck with a scotch in hand.

My favorite course was #4, but they were all wonderful. Our team did win the only skin of the day on #6 with an eagle on the par 4 5th hole. That paid most of our bar bill for the week. We played the course in September after Michael Campbell won The Open in June, but before the restoration done by Coore and Crenshaw in 2011. The fact that Michelle Wie played 72 holes without a three putt in 2014 US Women's Open is simply unbelievable to me. The greens at Pinehurst #2 were brutal. I hope to get back soon.

Memories of Pinehurst Resort

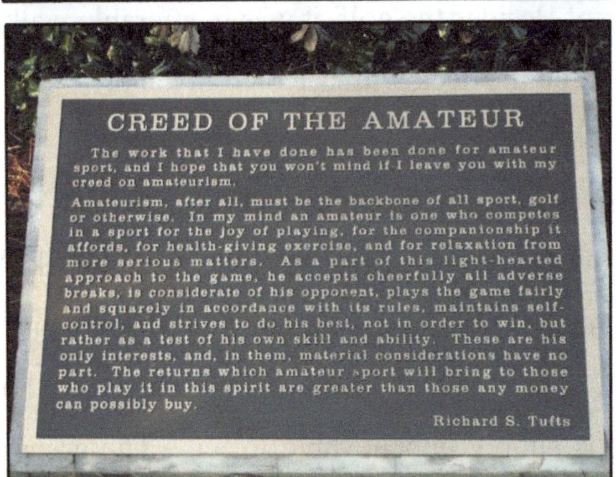

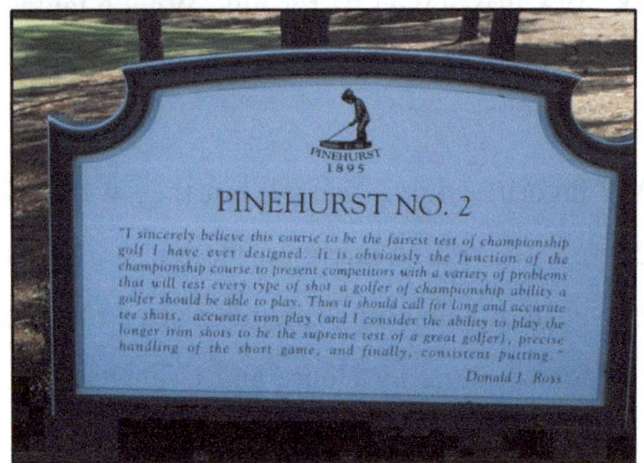

Our Team in the Pinehurst Pro-am

THE CENTENNIAL · PINEHURST No. 8 ·
11
547
PAR 5
HOLE #11
Young longleaf pines have
been planted bordering the
fairways to create future
habitat for the endangered
Red-cockaded Woodpecker.
Lands in the Sandhills are being
managed to recover this species
to non-endangered status.

Pinehurst #8

Tee Shots at the 160-yard par 3 6th hole at Pinehurst

North Dakota

We made it to Bowman, North Dakota as the third leg of our trip from Omaha, NE to Billings, MT and spent the night at the Bowman Lodge and Conference Center. Evidently the bars close at 8:45 pm, since we arrived slightly before 9 pm and were not able to get a drink or discuss the day's round at The Golf Club of Red Rock in South Dakota. From Bowman, we drove to Medora, North Dakota. Medora is a small town of 112 people (as of 2010), but with a rich history and a fabulous golf course.

President Theodore Roosevelt coined the term "bully pulpit" for the White House, meaning it was a great platform for which to influence opinion. The golf course in Medora decided to use the term also and with Teddy on horseback, a very cool logo.

Course: Bully Pulpit
Type: Public
Website:
https://medora.com/bullypulpit/
Location: Medora, ND
Phone: (701) 623-4653
Par 72. Yardage Played 6,655 (Gold)
Rating: 73.1/128

Bully Pulpit is part of the Theodore Roosevelt National Park and Little Missouri Grassland. The course is designed in a meadow on the Little Missouri River with holes that venture up into the badlands, this course offers players a variety of challenges from open grasslands & wooded areas, and of course, WOW corner up into the badlands. The changes in scenery and elevation make it a treat. The course played much longer than the scorecard yardages the day we were there since the course was wet with little roll.

In fact, after the round, we walked in the pro shop and asked if they had a T-shirt that proclaimed "I played the wrong Tees at Bully Pulpit." We played the Gold tees, listed at 6,655 yards, but the course felt like at least 8,000 yards.

Hole		1	2	3	4	5	6	7	8	9	OUT	10	11	12	13	14	15	16	17	18	IN	TOT	HCP	NET
Black	75.40/133	466	400	453	571	210	540	457	195	463	3755	448	517	203	318	404	161	451	503	406	3411	7166		
Gold	73.10/128	435	363	406	532	184	511	432	170	433	3466	397	485	195	291	395	153	421	478	374	3189	6655		
Blue	70.10/122	395	324	377	505	136	487	396	154	345	3119	333	462	173	261	323	135	395	457	322	2861	5980		
White	67.20/116	338	277	353	451	126	454	365	137	305	2806	307	424	149	232	273	134	345	393	265	2522	5328		
Red	68.30/113	321	252	340	408	97	408	334	111	280	2551	282	390	128	186	228	92	294	371	228	2199	4750		
PAR		4	4	4	5	3	5	4	3	4	36	4	5	3	4	4	3	4	5	4	36	72		
DATE:						SCORER:								ATTEST:										

The front nine plays toward the river and is relatively flat, but if you miss your target by more than a few yards, deep, deep, DEEP rough awaits and the ball may be lost. The holes have names evoking cheerful thoughts like "Black Gold" and "Peaceful Valley", but the course will bite you hard if you miss a shot. In late June, the large Cottonwood trees "snowing" on you on the holes near the river often make it a challenge to see your ball in the fairway and if you have allergies, be prepared with eye drops and medicine to help you breathe.

Once you emerge from beneath the bluff over the 13th green, the signature trio of holes deemed "The Badland Holes" await beginning on the 14th tee. Worked directly into the buttes, No. 14, while without a bunker, features a narrow landing area providing a challenge from the tee. As you make your way into the terrain, you will need an accurate approach, so choose your wedge wisely.

Next, the 15th is one of the most scenic and yet tricky par-3 holes you will ever play. The tee shot requires extreme accuracy as the 161-yard hole plays from a tee set atop a ridge to what seems like a microscopic green also set on a ridgetop. Overlooking the 15th green is the "Snarling Rock" just laughing at you for three putting after a fantastic tee shot to the green …

Views at Bully Pulpit Golf Course

Bully Pulpit is a very difficult course if played from the wrong set of tees or if you are having a wayward day with the Big Dog. Enjoy yourself and the scenery, remember, 90% of Golf is who you play with.

The Meadow and the Badlands at Bully Pulpit

168

Ohio

Ohio is home to seven US Presidents (8 if you count William Harrison who was living there when elected, but not a native). Additionally, more than 40 members of the professional golf tour, including Pete Dye, Gay Brewer, Denny Shute, Dow Finsterwald, Toney Penna, Jack Stranahan, Ben Curtis, Tom Weiskopf, John Cook, Harold Varner III, and of course, Jack Nicklaus call Ohio home. With more than 800 golf courses in Ohio, it is a great state for the sport. I have only played a few courses, the two most memorable being Toledo Country Club and Firestone's North Course.

Toledo Country Club was originally designed by British Open Champion Willie Park Jr. and was later redesigned by Arthur Hills. It is a heavily wooded parkland course with water on a few holes. I played there in a Charity Event and the course was spectacular.

Third Hole at Toledo Country Club and my tee gift

Firestone is the Crown Jewel in the Invited Clubs inventory of roughly 200 clubs in the United States. The South and North courses rank number one and two in Ohio, on Golfweek's 2023 list of the Best U.S. Courses You Can Play by State. The Fazio Course also made the list in the sixth spot, making all three layouts a must-play for golf enthusiasts.

Firestone also has a nine-hole putting course that's illuminated at night. It's a great place to prepare for a round or to simply hang out in the evening with a beverage.

Course: Firestone CC - North
Type: Resort
Website:
https://www.invitedclubs.com/clubs/firestone-country-club
Location: Akron, OH
Phone: (330) 644-8441
Par 72. Yardage Played 6,741 (Blue)
Rating: 73.1/130

We played the North Course for my nephew's high school graduation with my good friend Carl Erhart, aka "Mr. Humble." Marked by water on over half of the 18 holes, the North Course is designed and maintained to showcase Firestone's natural beauty. Since it opened in 1969, the North Course has hosted both the American Golf Classic and the World Series of Golf.

While the South Course at Firestone CC gets more notoriety, the North Course might be the best course on the property. Designed by Robert Trent Jones, Firestone North features an exciting blend of risk/reward par 5s and picturesque par x3s.

View back to the Water Tower from the Tee box from the 11th tee

The North course consistently delivers on conditioning, pace of play, and challenge. It doesn't receive the national recognition of the South Course, but it has a fantastic layout. Surprisingly, the few large ponds out front impact 10 of the 18 holes. It is really a great use of the water. There is also a hill that runs through the middle of the course that makes for a handful of interesting holes.

The North Course has an excellent group of tee shots during your round. There are doglegs in both directions that range from soft to severe. You'll drive it uphill and downhill. Additionally, you'll hit to some fairways that slope severely and some that are flat. The tee shots are fun at the North Course. Most holes feature a fairway bunker, and their placement shows just how impactful a single trap can be. Several holes also feature water on at least one side of the hole, which should be out of play, but it's amazing how quickly our drivers find it.

The 10th hole ends up being an awkward wedge into a water guarded green, the 11th is a mid- iron Par 3 completely over water, and the 12th, 13th and 14th are a few brute Par 4s. If given the choice, I would recommend starting on the front 9 to ease your way into the round.

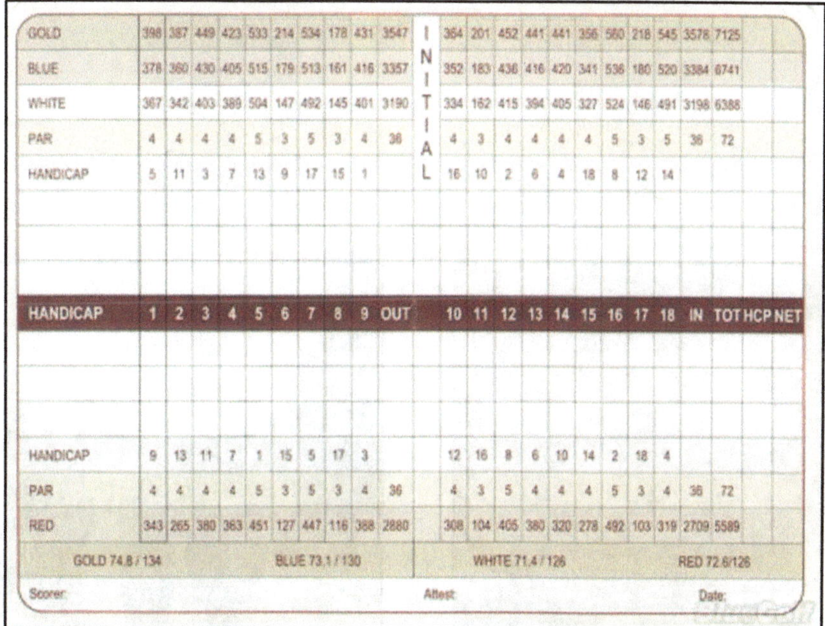

	1	2	3	4	5	6	7	8	9	OUT		10	11	12	13	14	15	16	17	18	IN	TOT	HCP	NET
GOLD	398	387	449	423	533	214	534	178	431	3547	I	364	201	452	441	441	356	560	218	545	3578	7125		
BLUE	378	360	430	405	515	179	513	161	416	3357	N	352	183	436	416	420	341	536	180	520	3384	6741		
WHITE	367	342	403	389	504	147	492	145	401	3190	I	334	162	415	394	405	327	524	146	491	3198	6388		
PAR	4	4	4	4	5	3	5	3	4	36	T	4	3	4	4	4	4	5	3	5	36	72		
HANDICAP	5	11	3	7	13	9	17	15	1		I	16	10	2	6	4	18	8	12	14				
											A													
HANDICAP	9	13	11	7	1	15	5	17	3		L	12	16	8	6	10	14	2	18	4				
PAR	4	4	4	4	5	3	5	3	4	36		4	3	5	4	4	4	5	3	4	36	72		
RED	343	265	380	363	451	127	447	116	388	2880		308	104	405	380	320	278	492	103	319	2709	5589		

GOLD 74.8 / 134	BLUE 73.1 / 130	WHITE 71.4 / 126	RED 72.6/126

Scorer: Attest: Date:

There are a lot of strategic decisions to be made off the tee and on the approach. Bad choices or errant shots can lead to big numbers. Getting out of the thick tree lines or missing in the Firestone Reservoir will load your card with penalty strokes.

Overall, the staff is always wonderful and the golf is on point. Paired with the great facilities at Firestone, it is always an enjoyable afternoon. Just take a walk through the clubhouse, or better yet, spend the night in one of the dorm-like rooms, say Tiger Woods? Highly recommend.

28 - TIGER WOODS

3 - JACK NICKLAUS

Oklahoma

Winstar World Resort in Thackerville, OK is just over the Red River at the Texas Border. The resort is less than 70 miles from DFW airport and holds the title as "the largest casino in the world" as of 2020 with 600,000 square feet of gaming space. We drove up from Austin for a buddy's weekend to play golf and enjoy the facilities at the resort. While the gambling was not successful for many of us, the food at the resort was excellent and the drinks were reasonably priced.

The Winstar Resort has two championship golf courses designed by PGA touring professional D.A. Weibring and his partner Steve Wolfard: Redbud and Scissortail. Both are very similar with open rolling links and sugary white bunkers, with undulating green complexes. There lies the difference from more urban parkland courses, there are few windbreaks and the wind is the primary defense of the two courses. Trust me, the wind blows hard in Oklahoma and a rainstorm can appear without a cloud in the sky. The courses have several water hazards, but it is the wind and deep rough that protect it from very low scores. I give the nod to Scissortail for more interesting shot values and design features.

Course: Winstar World Casino
Type: Resort
Website:
https://www.winstar.com/escape/destinations/winstar-golf-club/
Location: Thackerville, OK
Phone: (580) 276-4229
Par 72.
Redbud Yardage Played 6,679 (Blue)
Redbud Rating: 72.1/120

Scissortail Yardage Played 6,731 (Blue)
Scissortail Rating: 73.2/135

The Scissortail Course is the newer of the two. It opened in 2006 and can play between 5,000 and 7,200 yards. Scissortail is a gem of a layout with a variety of dogleg holes that force risk/reward decisions. The course was well maintained and had some pretty holes with the rolling terrain. Pick your tees wisely. The sugar white crystal bunkers are pristine requiring a firm strike through the ball to get it out and near the pin. The practice chipping area provides an excellent opportunity to improve this part of your game.

My favorite hole on the Scissortail course was the 13th. A 510-yard par 5 that was reachable with a drive in the fairway if you avoid the water on the right. Laying up with your second shot to leave a short wedge approach is also a good strategy.

Views at Scissortail and Redbud with our Group

Redbud is the original course at Winstar. It was redone in 2017 and is longer than Scissortail. So, if you like to hit the big dog hard, this would be a fun test! The fairways are huge, but be careful with your approach angles, because of the green complex contours. Missing the fairway in the first cut, will be flier time, the primary rough, is deep, penal stuff. Redbud has a links look to it and there is trouble on only a handful of holes. Five holes have water in play, but that water can be avoided fairly easily. It is a fun resort course to take your mind off the casino for a few hours.

My favorite hole at Redbud was the 380-yard par 4 5th. The tee shot had tall native grasses with water on the left side. The approach was to a slightly elevated green with bunkers on each side. Redbud ends with a par 3, which is not always fun, but in this case it fits the design and makes sense.

We all agreed to go back again and give these two courses another go.

Scissortail Golf Course

Redbud before and during the rainstorm

Oregon

Oregon is a beautiful state. The Oregon coastline abounds with incredible views and the cascade mountain range is stunning. Silver Falls State Park, Crater Lake and Mount Hood are awesome natural wonders. From the Snake River in the north to Klamath Falls in the south and from the Pacific Ocean on the west to the eastern plains, Oregon is a stunning place. It is also the only state with an official state nut! The official state nut of Oregon is the hazelnut. The hazelnut is also known as the filbert.

In addition to being the United States leader in registered Ghost Towns (with more than 80), the beaver state contains more than 200 golf courses. I have played golf in Portland, Salem, Eugene, Coos Bay, Bandon and Bend. They were all fun and interesting. For the record, I have only been to one Ghost Town, Idiotville.

In Portland we played The Reserve Vineyards which was home to the Fred Myer Challenge hosted by touring professional Peter Jacobson from 1986 until 2002. We also played the Witch Hollow

Course at Pumpkin Ridge, thanks to a friend of Dr. Dubois. Witch Hollow is where Tiger Woods won his Third US Amateur in 1996. Both courses were challenging and fun.

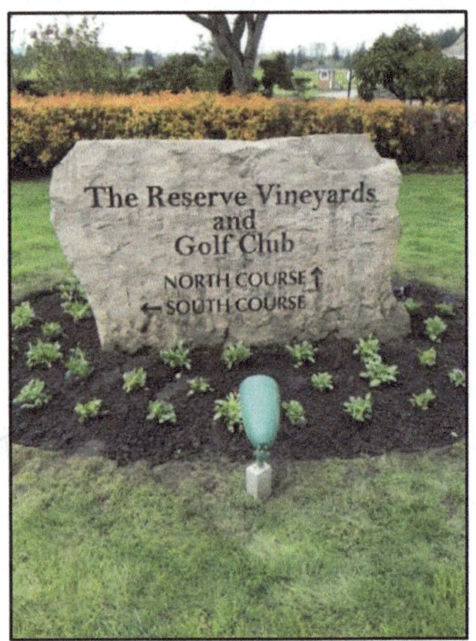

Reserve Vineyards and Witch Hollow

Near Eugene, we played an interesting course, Pine Ridge. Pine Ridge is not a five-star club. It has chickens roaming the course, large (very large) trees in the middle of the fairways, and a river running through it to challenge you.

Views from Pine Ridge Golf Course Near Eugene

Obviously, Bandon Dunes resort is the star of Oregon. Six courses (Bandon Dunes, Bandon Trails, Pacific Dunes, Old MacDonald, Sheep Ranch and The Preserve (13 hole par three)); Good lodging, incredible service; excellent food and good beer. Caddies that know golf and what makes a round enjoyable for the guest, fun banter, good stories, and help to hit a career shot or make a putt here and there. I have been to Bandon Dunes four times and am ready to go back tomorrow if someone invites me. It is a special place.

Course: Bandon Dunes
Type: Resort
Website: https://www.bandondunesgolf.com
Location: Bandon, OR
Phone: (855) 220-6710
Par 72.
Bandon Dunes 6,221 yards played. 71.1/133
Pacific Dunes 6,142 yards played. 70.8/135
Bandon Trails 6,249 yards played. 72.0/137
Old McDonald 6,320 yards played.
71.4/127
Sheep Ranch 6,245 yards played. 70.0/116
Preserve 1,609 yards played

Waiting on the First Tee at Bandon Dunes

If you talk to a hundred people that have played Bandon Dunes about their personal rankings, you will likely get Pacific Dunes or Bandon Dunes as #1. A few will pick Bandon Trails and very few would choose Old MacDonald or Sheep Ranch. The Sheep Ranch has stunning views with a lot of photo opportunities, but the golf is vanilla. Old Mac has the iconic ghost tree, is wide open, with big undulating greens. It is very fun. Bandon Trails is an inland course that paid for its construction by selling the lumber from the trees removed to make the course. It is an outstanding design that requires good golf shots but is missing the "WOW!" Views to get it a #1 ranking on the property. Golf Digest and Golf Magazine both rank Pacific Dunes over Bandon Dunes and I agreed with this after my first visit. But after four trips, I now put Bandon Dunes on top. I think the shot values are outstanding and the layout is just a little less penal and more fun. The bunkers and gorse at Pacific require precise drives and approaches and limit the options to play chip shots around the greens.

The 16th Hole at Bandon Dunes is a short par four (360 yards) with a gorge that gouges into the hole not too far beyond the tee box and then a barranca ledge further down the hole near the driving zone. Carrying both hazards takes a decent drive, but nothing overly heroic. The approach shot into the green is both stunningly gorgeous and treacherous with the ocean crashing on the beach just beyond the cliff edge behind the putting surface. My favorite hole on the property.

Bandon Dunes #16

At 150 yards, the 11th hole at Pacific Dunes is the definition of a postcard hole: short, fun, and attractive. Bring your camera. It is the second of back-to-back par 3s, well above the Pacific Ocean with deep natural bunkers in front and right of the smallest green on the entire course. The winds off the ocean wreak havoc with a ball hit high with a spinning short iron.

Pacific Dunes #11

My favorite hole at Bandon Trails is the 5th. It plays 135 yards to an enormous undulating green leading to lots of three putts. The bunkers in front, swallow golf balls with a Shrek-like appetite.

Bandon Trails #5

My favorite hole on Old MacDonald is the 535-yard par 5, 15th. The hole is named "Westward Ho!" and it takes players straight towards the Pacific Ocean by playing from one dune to another though a very wide fairway. A bunker complex separates the 15th and 16th holes and can be a factor to consider depending on the time of year and wind. The approach shot is uphill and sometimes blind. I was lucky enough to hole my third shot for eagle here on one visit playing from one knee up the slope. I didn't see it but heard the cheers from my partner and the jeers from our opponents.

Old MacDonald #15

The 13-hole par 3 Preserve course is a gem. The shortest hole is 60 yards and the longest 150. It is a great way to spend a couple of hours playing an eightsome with your buddies enjoying the views and paying for all birdies. The 13th is straight downhill 110 yards. In our group the rule was that the hole must be played with either a driver or a putter. In our case, we opted for the putter and Jon almost aced it, hitting the pin and stopping a couple of inches away. We all paid him.

Views from The Preserve

The Sheep Ranch features more holes on the ocean than any other at the resort which is the opposite experience Coore & Crenshaw were given when they designed Bandon Trails 15 years earlier. The Sheep Ranch has so many picturesque holes that you can literally take photos all day long. My favorite hole on the course is the par 4 17th. It is short, 330 yards, but has a visually challenging tee shot over the beach and a flip wedge approach to a smallish green guarded by the "Gallow" tree and the ocean on the left. Missing right leaves a delicate chip out of gnarly rough.

Sheep Ranch #17 from the tee and at the Green

The greens at all six of the Bandon Resort courses are huge—some 60 or more yards deep—bring your best lag putting game! Many bunkers have stairs to enter and exit because they're that steep and require high soft shots to get close. The wind! Oh, the wind howls in the afternoon, sometimes moving putts as much as a foot offline! Never try to overpower the wind; it wins every time. Swing Easy and Accept the Extra Distance! Hit several more clubs into the wind or choose to use a hybrid or putter from 40 yards off the green. This is Links Golf!

Two excellent reads before you get to Bandon are <u>Dream Golf: The Making of Bandon Dunes</u> by Stephen Goodwin and <u>The Making of Pacific Dunes</u> by Tom Doak. The first book is about Mike Keiser's dream for the property and the construction of the courses with fantastic pictures of the teams that built them. The second book delves deep into details about Pacific Dunes including analysis of the wind speed and direction at different times of the year, vegetation, and different routings that were considered. Both books are fun for a golf nut!

Views from Bandon Courses

The Gorse on the course shines brightly in the spring and frames many shots. Do not hit into it. It hurts and is difficult to get out. Take a caddie! They help navigate the bumps and slopes of links, avoid the gorse and are wizards in the blustery winds. They guide my club choice and provide reads on the greens that you would not believe. Trust your Caddie! They are key to the Bandon experience and are worth every penny.

Views of the Gorse in April

The well positioned "ghost" trees at Old MacDonald and the Sheep Ranch make for wonderful photo opportunities. My caddie told me that these trees were moved to the current locations to beautify the properties. They did it very well.

Ghost Trees at Bandon, Old MacDonald on the left, Sheep Ranch on the Right

My caddies and my playing partners always make Bandon a memorable experience. I asked my good friend Blake, who has played with me in 26 states at last count, what was his favorite thing about our Bandon Trips. He said, "The most memorable thing was getting caught in the hail storm. The most fun was drinking and playing pool and inventing dice games in the bar after the round with our buddies." 90% of golf is who you play. Traveling with Blake is always fun.

Friends and Caddies at Bandon Dunes

Friends at Bandon

My good friend Pat once told me he could not go on another golf trip with me because our trip to Bandon could never by topped. We had amazing weather, incredible golf, and a great group of compadres from Austin and Dallas to stroll the fairways. If you can get there, you should, and take some good friends.

My Friend Pat at Pacific Dunes

Pennsylvania

Pennsylvania, the Keystone State, is wide. It is a 5.5-hour drive from Philadelphia to Pittsburgh on I-76, a little over 300 miles. Feel free to stop in Punxsutawney and say Hello to Phil, the United States most notable ground hog, just 84 miles east of Pittsburgh. It's often difficult to remember 2nd place, but Pennsylvania was the second state in the United States after Delaware.   There is a lot of excellent golf in Pennsylvania including Oakmont Country Club and Latrobe Country Club. Oakmont is known for their fast greens and picturesque "Church pew" bunkers on the 428-yard 3rd hole, while Latrobe is known as the home of Arnold and Winnie Palmer.

For a short time in my professional career, I was a "Visiting Industrial Scholar" to Carnegie Mellon University in Pittsburgh. While there I was able to play several courses in the Pittsburgh area. I had reciprocal privileges at two of them: Diamond Run Golf Club and Treesdale Golf and Country Club through my home club in Austin. Since it was inexpensive to play those courses, I played them most often. Both are fun and interesting courses. Treesdale is a 27-hole Arnold Palmer design that gives three different challenges to the golfer with substantial hazards and some forced carries, it is a fun test. Many professional athletes are members there and play in some of the member events which is always enjoyable.

Course: Treesdale CC – Groves/Lakes
Type: Private
Website:
https://www.invitedclubs.com/clubs/treesdale-golf-country-club
Location: Gibsonia, PA
Phone: (724) 625-2220
Par 72. Yardage Played 6,614 (Blue)
Rating: 72.4/143

My good friend, Carl ("Mr. Humble") was a member at Treesdale and thought it the better course with a great pub. Mr. Humble believed the Grove to Lakes rotation was the most challenging and fun. The course is all bent grass with greens usually fast. From the men's tee, the slope is low 140's and tougher from the tips in the upper 140's and a 74+ stroke rating. Not a course to whack a driver on every hole. Treesdale forces different shots since many holes require a layup or carry over the water. The par 3's on the Grove nine are guarded by bunkers, while both of them on the Lakes nine require full carries to clear the water/marsh. There is little room to miss on any of them. It's Pennsylvania golf, so there are hills and side sloping fairways. Not a course to walk. The carts are gas since a battery would not make it 18 holes.

Diamond run is about 10-15 miles away and is an 18-hole track that runs through a neighborhood. Mr. Humble played it a few times since they had a match play cup between the two clubs. I played it a handful of times.

Course: Diamond Run CC
Type: Private
Website:
https://www.invitedclubs.com/clubs/diamond-run-golf-club
Location: Sewickley, PA
Phone: (412) 741-2020
Par 72. Yardage Played 6,490 (Blue)
Rating: 72.1/134

Diamond Run was my personal favorite because of the undulating fairways and fantastic greens. It is a Gary Player design. Certainly, the best Gary Player Design that I have ever played as most of the course is in front of you and there are only a couple of quirky shots. The Gary Player designs that I have played had a quirky aspect either in routing or shot views. Arnold Palmer designs, on the other hand, provide golfers with straightforward targets and clear routings. Diamond Run has wide fairways and large greens that fit well in the western Pennsylvania landscape. The course is not overly long, we played it at about 6,500 yards, but it tips out at 6,900. The tee shots can be challenging, and the greens were in amazing shape and were running about an 11 on the Stimpmeter. Keeping your drive on the fairway is paramount as the rough can be US Open deep in some places. There are some out-of-bounds that come into play as well. Only one hole really has water in play (15) and it is a beautiful and long par 4. Two of the Par 5's provide a good chance at a birdie (9 & 14) and the other Par 5's (3 & 12 & 17) are much more challenging. There is a plaque on the 15th hole declaring the final four holes as the "most challenging and scenic finishing holes in western Pennsylvania," which says a lot with Oakmont and Latrobe CC just down the road.

Views at Diamond Run Golf Course

Rhode Island

Rhode Island is a small place. In the movie "Arthur" Dudley Moore was explaining what a small place was and he commented "Rhode Island would kill it in a war." Not sure why, but that line always made me laugh and has stuck with me since 1981. As for golf, Rhode Island has only 55 golf courses. I played "The Met" in 2020 before the Golf Digest article was published about Brad Faxon saving his childhood course and then being sued by the members for fraud.

Metacomet Country club was a very short (6,200 yards) Donald Ross design that had incredibly fast undulating greens, mean bunkers and left you scratching your head about how to play it. I played with clients from a major bank in the area and unfortunately have no pictures of my own, so I am using some published by @worldgolfer with his permission. I agree with his review, completely. (https://worldgolfer.blog/2016/10/13/review-metacomet-country-club/)

South Carolina

South Carolina, the Palmetto State, was known as the Iodine State, and even said so on the license plates in the 1930's. Palmetto trees are way prettier for a flag, anyway. According to preservation society of Charleston, the first game of golf played in the U.S. took place in Charleston, SC in 1743.

Myrtle Beach or Hilton Head? Always the question when heading to South Carolina. Myrtle Beach claims the title of "Golf Capital of the World" with more than 80 courses within just a few miles. Hilton Head Island's more than 23 championship courses include oceanfront layouts as well as parkland and links-style courses. Charleston and Bluffton are also home to a number of popular courses created by top golf course architects attracted by South Carolina's weather, natural beauty and great beaches. There are more than 350 golf courses in South Carolina! It is about 220 miles between Myrtle Beach and Hilton Head. Kiawah Island is in between the two … Golfer's heaven. If you are going to do a buddy's trip on the east coast, South Carolina rocks it.

Personally, I am a Hilton Head fan. My buddies and I rented a condo on the 13th hole of the Heron Point course in Hilton Head in early February.

We played Harbortown (home of the RBC Heritage Classic on the PGA Tour), the Ocean Course at Kiawah (Home of the Ryder Cup and Three PGA Championships), Heron Point, Haig Point and the Country Club of Hilton Head. It was spectacular. We had after round drinks and seafood at Hudson's on the Docks and went to dinner at a fantastic Italian restaurant, Stellini's.

View of our condo on the 13th at Heron Point

After Round Drinks at Hudson's and at Haig Point

Harbour Town and the Ocean Course at Kiawah did not disappoint. They were fantastic tracks that lived up to their rankings. At Harbour Town, the starter actually let us play a fivesome, because we were the only group on the course! At Kiawah we were broke into two groups and paired with other players. Harbour Town hosts the RBC Heritage Classic each year on the PGA Tour. It is the weekend after the Masters and has had some wonderful champions, including Arnold Palmer, Jack Nicklaus, Hale Irwin, Johnny Miller, Nick Faldo, Davis Love III, Boo Weekly and Jordan Spieth. The Ocean Course is just plain hard. It has a slope rating of 155 and, in my opinion, that is too low. The "War by the Shore" Ryder cup matches there were epic. Rory McIlroy won the PGA Championship by 12 shots in 2012 and Phil Mickelson became the Oldest Major winner at Kiawah in 2021 right after turning 50 years old! It was stunning walking back to the "Tournament Tees" and looking at the small areas these guys had to hit their drivers into, and the carry distances were jaw dropping. If the wind was blowing at all, I could never make the fairway on many holes. Always fun to play where the big boys play…

The Group at Harbour Town and Blake and Me at Kiawah

My favorite course of the trip, however, was Haig Point. We had an enjoyable 30-to-40-minute ferry ride from Hilton Head to Daufuskie Island. Daufuskie is a small private island with one awesome golf course. There are no cars on the island, so a representative from the club picked us up at the dock and shuttled us down to the golf clubhouse.

Ferry Ride to Daufuskie Island and view of the Harbortown Lighthouse from the 5th Green

Haig Point is a private Rees Jones Design containing 20 holes. We were able to get a tee time through reciprocal privileges with our home course in Austin. Several fantastic par 3s and views of the sound right across from the Harbour Town Lighthouse. The course was immaculate, the wildlife was everywhere, gators, herons, squirrels, mice, snakes… everything for which you could ask. The best thing? Our group had the whole course to ourselves. In fact, some staff came in to open the bar and restaurant for us early when we finished our round! Talk about service! The drinks and food were excellent and the ferry ride back to our condo was very relaxed.

Course: Haig Point
Type: Private
Website: https://haigpoint.com/club-life/golf/
Location: Daufuskie Island, SC
Phone: (843) 686-2000
Par 72. Yardage Played 6,330 (White)
Rating: 71.3/131

Both sides open with a few holes through the trees that then open up to the Calibogue Sound. The 4th hole is a dogleg right par 5 that gets very narrow at the approach with severe bunkering to penalize mis-hit approaches. The 5th is a beautiful par 3 of 165 yards with a HUGE green that looks small from the tee. The 10th is one of my most memorable holes. A 390-yard par 4 with large gators hanging out near the water's edge of the sharp dogleg right. It is very tempting to try to cut a large chunk of the water, but I recommend a safer play leaving you a good approach to a well bunkered green. The par 5 14th has been ranked as one of the 99 best holes in the United States. The green on the 14th sits on a high piece of ground between two wetland areas requiring a precision approach. The 15th and 17th are just stunning one-shot holes that require a camera as much as a 5 iron. Taking the boardwalk back to the tee and strolling along the marsh grasses is just fun.

Every course we played on this trip had Alligators sunning themselves in the fairways or sleeping in ponds. A couple were too close for comfort for me, but my friend Larry had no issues walking up to them and tapping them back into the pond.

Larry helping an Alligator back into the pond at Haig Point and a Gator in the Marsh at Hilton Head

Views at Haig Point

Views at Haig Point

Hilton Head Wildlife

South Dakota

South Dakota is one of the least densely populated states in the United States. As of 2022 slightly less than 1 million people live within its 77,000 square miles. Arguably the two most recognizable landmarks in South Dakota are Mount Rushmore and the town of Sturgis, where a large motorcycle rally is held each year in August.

My friends and me visiting Mt. Rushmore

A short twenty-minute ride north from Mount Rushmore (and 40 minutes south of Sturgis) is The Golf Club at Red Rock. Ranked as one the best residential courses in the United States by Golfweek and rated the #1 Public Course in South Dakota out of the 77 that are available.

<table>
<tr><td>
Course: The Golf Club at Red Rock
Type: Public
Website:
https://www.golfclubatredrock.com
Location: Rapid City, SD
Phone: (605) 718-4710
Par 72. Yardage Played 6,567 (Blue)
Rating: 71.0/138
</td></tr>
</table>

The practice area was very fun. Two large blow-up chipping targets, a Dragon and a Kangaroo were available to practice flying your chip shots into their pouches. The practice tee had several levels to hit from and four green complexes with flags available for targets as well as bunkers to support better alignment. This would be a fun place to practice and learn.

The Driving Range at The Golf Club at Red Rock

The course itself is maintained in excellent condition. It features lush fairways, surrounded by native grasses and tall ponderosa pine trees. The course sits at 3,200 feet above sea level giving a little extra distance to your drives, but with links-style bunkers and large green complexes it can be a stern test.

Dramatic elevation changes and several blind shots make The Golf Club at Red Rock difficult for a visitor to find the correct line off the tee or to the green. The first hole is an inviting par 4 that is severely downhill, many players believe they can drive the green, but beware… miss right in the deep fescue or short into the greenside bunker and you will have a challenging par thanks to a very difficult green.

The uphill par 5 second is a definite three shot hole. A large mound on the left and a huge tree on the right frame this hole and force you to shape the ball one way or another on your second shot. The green is elevated leaving you blind to a middle or back pin location… it is a challenge.

The downhill sixth is a 220-yard par 3 that plunges more than 100 feet to the green making it play more like 175 yards. A pot bunker on the right and a virtual forest 15 yards left of the green leave no room for error. There is a ridge that bisects the green making putting very difficult if you are not positioned correctly.

The 10th hole has a lovely view across a pond to the green, it is a very nice hole. The wildlife on the course along with a solid set of closing holes make the overall experience very enjoyable. The 13th was also memorable. Teeing off through a chute of trees over a barranca to a open fairway with tall native grasses on the right. The green is guarded by a large bunker on the right with deep grass surrounding the bunker… definitely better to be in the sand than the gnarly deep grass.

Views at The Golf Club of Red Rock

Tennessee

Tennessee borders eight other U.S. States. The Volunteer state is also the birthplace of Cotton Candy, the Moon Pie, and Mountain Dew. Staples for the kid in all of us. The Grand Ole Opry, Memphis Blues, and Graceland have played a major role in the United States music scene with Graceland being the second most visited house in the United States after the White House. Unfortunately, the golf scene is not very strong. There are 176 courses in Tennessee, with only The Honors Course (near Chattanooga) ranked in the top 100 in the US.

So far, I have only played one course in Tennessee. It was not a good course but had a nice logo. The 18-hole "Quail Ridge" course at the Quail Ridge Golf Course facility in Bartlett, Tennessee (near Memphis) features 6,600 yards of golf from the longest tees for a par of 70. The course rating is 72.6 and it had a slope rating of 127 on Bermuda grass. The Quail Ridge golf course opened in 1994 designed by David Pfaff, a former Pete Dye Assistant. Unlike the typical Memphis flat terrain, Quail Ridge golf course has some rolling hills and minor elevation changes. Tree lined fairways, seven lakes and a winding creek give Quail Ridge a rustic feel that is unparalleled in the Memphis area public golf market.

Course: Quail Ridge
Type: Public
Website: None
Location: Bartlett, TN
Phone: (901) 386-6951
Par 70. Yardage Played 6349 (Blue)
Rating: 70.9/126

My buddies and I chose this course sight unseen because we were in Mississippi and wanted to play in Tennessee and go to Graceland. We could not have made a worse choice. Although we did get a good deal on the round. Upon arrival we entered the clubhouse and a young man sat behind the register. We said we had made a tee time and he said "Are you guys seniors?" and we answered in the affirmative. He only charged us $25 including cart and a hat. I said "Really?" And he said yeah. So, we took the cart key and went to load up. Our third player was charged $65 because he stopped to go to the bathroom … you snooze you lose evidently.

The layout, architecture, and shot shapes are decent, but the fairways needed some love. They were mostly dirt. The greens were bumpy and hard as rocks. The 13th hole was a memorable 170-yard par 3 over water and 15th was a short par 5 that was a fun hole to play.

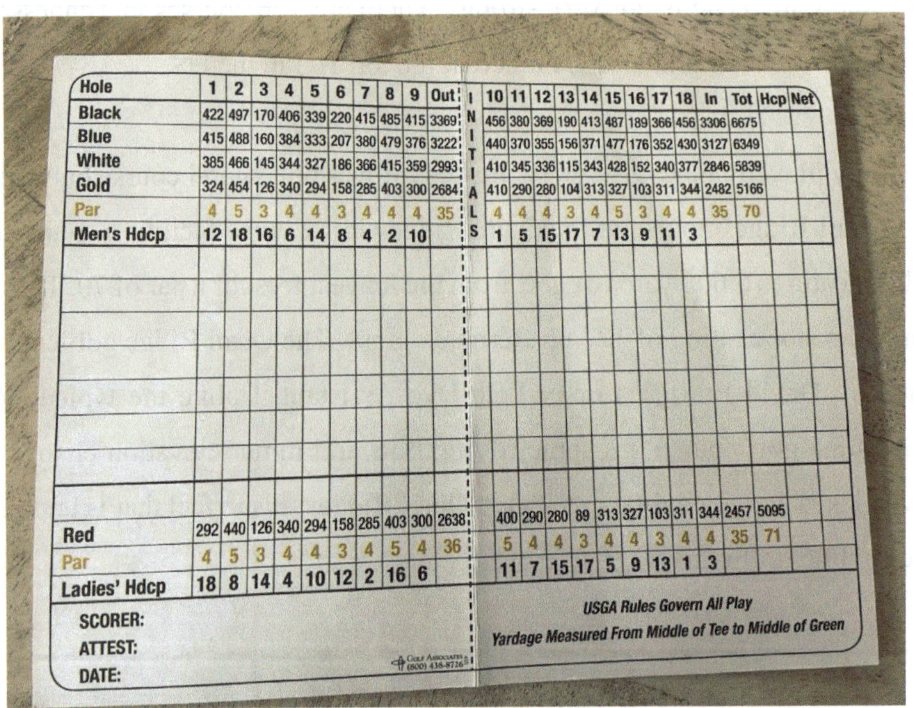

Hole	1	2	3	4	5	6	7	8	9	Out		10	11	12	13	14	15	16	17	18	In	Tot	Hcp	Net
Black	422	497	170	406	339	220	415	485	415	3369		456	380	369	190	413	487	189	366	456	3306	6675		
Blue	415	488	160	384	333	207	380	479	376	3222		440	370	355	156	371	477	176	352	430	3127	6349		
White	385	466	145	344	327	186	366	415	359	2993		410	345	336	115	343	428	152	340	377	2846	5839		
Gold	324	454	126	340	294	158	285	403	300	2684		410	290	280	104	313	327	103	311	344	2482	5166		
Par	4	5	3	4	4	3	4	4	4	35		4	4	4	3	4	5	3	4	4	35	70		
Men's Hdcp	12	18	16	6	14	8	4	2	10			1	5	15	17	7	13	9	11	3				
Red	292	440	126	340	294	158	285	403	300	2638		400	290	280	89	313	327	103	311	344	2457	5095		
Par	4	5	3	4	4	3	4	5	4	36		5	4	4	3	4	4	3	4	4	35	71		
Ladies' Hdcp	18	8	14	4	10	12	2	16	6			11	7	15	17	5	9	13	1	3				

Views from Quail Ridge Golf Course

Overall, though, we had more fun at Graceland than we did playing Quail Ridge. Peter bought us the VIP package which turned out to be a great call. Lots of line skipping with interesting talks from the hostess and transportation around the property. I need to play more rounds in Tennessee to give it another chance or two.

My Friends, Blake and Peter, at Graceland

Texas

Texas is larger than any country in Europe. The King Ranch, headquartered in Kingsville, Texas, is 825,000 acres and touches six Texas counties. Texas also has their own power grid, separate from the two that support the rest of the United States. It is also the home to the largest Bat population in North America with 20 million bats living in Bracken cave just outside San Antonio.

As the saying goes, "I wasn't born in Texas, but I got here as fast as I could." I moved to the Clear Lake area of Houston in 1984 to work on the Space Shuttle program as a NASA contractor. Best job I ever had. Great team, simple goal, exciting execution. In 1997, I moved to the Austin area and joined the Lakeway Golf Club. Golf in Texas was (and still is) a challenge for me. Narrow, rock hard fairways with Bermuda greens and a lot of bare lies to chip from often leave you scratching your head. You learn different shots in Texas, low burners to keep it under the wind, "Texas Wedge" or Hybrid putts off the hard pan around the greens, driver off the deck under the trees and through the cactus. The key saying is "Swing Easy and Accept the Extra Distance."

I have played many courses all over the state, from Lajitas in Terlingua to Beaumont Country Club as well as from South Padre Island Golf Club to Ross Rogers in Amarillo. Austin, Houston, Dallas-Ft. Worth, San Antonio, and El Paso all have wonderful golf. Although in the 2023 list of Golf Digest top 100 courses in the United States, Texas registered only 1 course. One course in the Top 100… This is shocking to me. I think Colonial, Dallas National, Austin Golf Club, Escondido, the UT Golf Club and Spanish Oaks are all worthy of inclusion (and these are ones that I have played) ahead of Old MacDonald at Bandon Dunes which is number 72. I'm sure others that I have not played BlueJack National, for example, should be included. I have played several of the courses that host PGA Tour events in Texas, including Colonial, Memorial Park in Houston, TPC Woodlands, TPC San Antonio, La Cantera, TPC McKinney Ranch and Las Colinas among others that are very nice and entertaining tracks. So far, I have played 159 out of the 907 courses in Texas. I will play more.

Course: Live Oak
Type: Private
Website:
https://www.invitedclubs.com/clubs/the-hills-country-club/golf/live-oak-course
Location: Lakeway, TX
Phone: (512) 263-7173
Par 72. Yardage Played 6339 (Blue)
Rating: 72.1/126

I live on the 18th green at the Live Oak Course in Lakeway, Texas, a suburb near Austin, so this is the course I choose to highlight. Live Oak is part of The Hills of Lakeway, a 72-hole facility with two Jack Nicklaus and two Leon Howard Designs. Live Oak is one of the Leon Howard courses. I have been a member of The Hills of Lakeway for more than 25 years.

The Live Oak course is unique and certainly not everyone's cup of tea. There are only three bunkers on the entire course, all on the 9th hole short and right of the green. They were installed in 2007 along with a split rail fence to beautify the drive into the club house, prior to that, the course was void of sand. The signature hole is number 12, nicknamed "Jaws," which ranges from 110 yards to 204 yards over a barranca. Another good hole is the 380-yard par 4 5th. This hole usually requires a layup off the tee because of large trees and a pond that guards the direct path to the hole. An uphill second shot to a left-to-right sloping green complex challenges you after a well-executed tee shot.

"Jaws" 200-yard par 3

Live Oak #5 looking back from the Green

The 10th hole is a short dog leg right par 4. Longer hitters launch it over the houses on the right and go for the green. We shorter players hit it about 200 yards down the fairway and hope it does not bound into the lateral hazard on the left off the big hill. We then have 110 yards onto the green.

The 18th is a 440-yard par 4. It is a narrow, uphill hole with a two-tier green that challenges even the best players. It plays much longer than the yardage. It is a spectacular finishing hole because you can score anywhere between a 2 (I holed out a 4 hybrid here for eagle once in a club tournament) to an 8 (hit it OB right and then in the hazard left on the second).

Tee shot on #10   *Tee Shot on #18*

The Live Oak course is interesting because it has five dogleg left holes, five dogleg right holes, and four straight away holes, to go with a good mix of par 3s. It really does require you to work the ball or hit it very high or very low over or under the hundreds of very old Live Oak trees on the property. The course hosted the Monday qualifier for the Kinko's Classic (a Champions Tour event) in 2003. Out of the 70+ professionals that tried to qualify that day only two professionals played Live Oak under par. In fact, twenty plus professionals scored greater than 90, another 14 withdrew. It is not a pushover. BTW, Hale Irwin won the Kinko's Classic that year at The Hills Signature Course (considered the best of the four courses at our club).

In 2004, I was lucky enough to be invited to play in the Kinko's Classic Pro-Am with George Archer at Live Oak. He was an incredibly nice man. It was his 999th professional tournament and the last event he ever played. George practiced his chipping on every tee box while we waited to hit and told us stories of his playing days and his childhood in Gilroy, CA. He said his favorite course was Shadow Creek in Las Vegas. George told us how incredible it felt to win the Masters in 1969 and how happy he was to respond to the San Francisco golf writer who said he was too tall to win on tour! (He won 13 times on tour and 43 professional tournaments). The format of our Pro-Am was a four-person Shamble with 80% handicap of the amateurs. Our team shot 49, yes 49! To win the Pro-Am by 6 shots. We won a Crystal Scotch Decanter with four scotch glasses and a golf bag for the first-place finish! One of my best golf memories!

Another fond memory is winning the Live Oak Player's Championship back-to-back in 2017 and 2018. Luckily for me the better players in the club either did not play or had a bad day. I was able to shoot 71 and 70 respectively to earn the championship flags.

I have grown to like Texas golf and especially my home course, it is different than other places. Texas golf does not get the love it deserves from the nation in the various rankings.

Finally, we have a pleasant set of wildlife visiting our golf course on a regular basis. Here's a few photos that I've captured in our players gallery through the years.

Utah

Utah was nicknamed "The Beehive State" in 1848 with the state motto of "Industry" because early founders from the Church of Latter-day Saints (i.e., Mormons) believed that the beehive was synonymous with industry and perseverance, two values that the church founders praised. The state's five national parks are stunning landscapes to visit and learn about how the earth has changed over time. The Sundance Film Festival in Park City is a fun time for discovering independent films and the 30,000 acres of salt at the Bonneville Salt Flats provides the location for land speed racing. Golf is not high on the Utah priority list.

There are, however, nearly 140 golf courses in Utah with both desert and mountain terrain that provides a wide variety of golf to be played. A great friend of mine moved to Salt Lake City in the early 1990s and I have had the pleasure of visiting him and his lovely wife a couple of times. Salt Lake City sits at an elevation of just over 4,200 feet above sea level. This gives you a few extra yards on well hit high shots.

Course: Nibly Park
Type: Public
Website: https://www.slc-golf.com/nibleypark/
Location: Salt Lake City, UT
Phone: (801) 483-5418
Par 34. Yardage Played 2895(Blue)
Rating: 65.0/110

In August 1994, Steve Bayer and I had planned to play golf in the canyon north of Salt Lake City, but very high winds (30-40 mph) scared us away. So, we went to Nibly Park Golf Course in downtown Salt Lake. Nibly Park is the oldest public golf course in Utah and is a charming nine-hole layout. It is very short, playing just under 3,000 yards from the back tees, but offered a unique and enjoyable experience. As a public course it known for inexpensive golf and a nice walk. There are breathtaking views of the surrounding mountains, but Nibley Park is surrounded on three sides by city streets, with traffic noise coming into play on 5 of the 9 holes. The course is perfect for beginners looking to develop their golf skills and for seasoned players seeking a quick, relaxing round.

Hole 5 is the only par 5 at Nibly Park. It presents golfers with an intriguing challenge. This hole measures only 450 yards and features a slight dogleg to the left. A tree-lined fairway demands accuracy off the tee, as errant shots can easily find trouble. A stream meanders through the fairway at about 90 yards from the green and all the way down to the left side of the green. The green is tiered with a slope from back to front.

Hole 5 at Nibly Park

On Hole 9 golfers face a picturesque par-3 that measures approximately 130 yards. The tee box offers stunning views of the nearby mountains. A water hazard guarding the front and left side of the green adds complexity to the hole. There is about 15 yards of landing area between the front of the green and the water. A bunker protects the entire front right side of the green. Most pin placements will be directly over this bunker making this shot a little nerve-racking. The green is small and undulated. Trees line the backside of the green creating a cathedral feel. Players must select the right club and execute a precise shot to navigate the water and land safely on the green.

It's not only a test of skill but also a chance to take in the natural beauty that makes Nibly Park Golf Course a favorite among local golfers.

Hole 9 at Nibly Park

Nibly Park Golf Course is a destination for those looking for a quick round of golf in a tranquil, natural setting, and holes like 5 and 9 contribute to its unique and enjoyable character. It is an inexpensive short, fun nine hole municipal course to learn the game and hang out with friends. Overall, we had a very enjoyable day at this Salt Lake City gem. The photos were provided by my good friend, Steve Bayer.

Views of Nibley Park Golf Course

Vermont

Vermont is known for maple syrup (produces the most in the United States), teddy bears (Vermont Teddy Bears produce 500,000 per year), covered bridges (most per square mile in the United States) and ice cream (Ben and Jerry's Cherry Garcia is a personal favorite). Like Texas, Vermont was once a separate country. As far as golf, both Keegan Bradley and Patty Sheehan were born in Vermont and went on to win major championships.

Fox Run was originally opened in 1969 as a 9-hole executive golf course located on the 150-acre Moore Family dairy farm in Ludlow, Vermont. The course was bulldozed in 1999 and a new course Okemo Valley Golf Club was opened. Okemo Valley course was managed by Jim Remy, Past President of the PGA of America for almost 20 years until it was sold again in 2021 and the name was changed back to Fox Run. We played in the middle of this transition, we made our tee time at Okemo Valley, but when we arrived at the course it was called Fox Run! Imagine our surprise coming from Texas and looking for Okemo Valley and all the signage said Fox Run.

Once we found the pro shop, it was a fantastic experience! There are few courses that have exceeded my expectations more than Fox Run. The course is short, 6,500 yards par 70 from the tips, but it is no pushover. It is a mountain golf course with tall native grasses and beautiful tall trees framing your shots. The course undulations, leaving you to play the ball above, below, and rarely level with your feet. Course Architect Steve Durkee designed and built a course that fits perfectly in its environment

Fox Run has received accolades, including a five-star rating from the New England Golf Guide, named a Top 50 Course in America from 2003-2007 by Golf for Women, Golfweek Best Courses You Can Play and was a qualifier site for the U.S. Women's Amateur Public Links Championship.

Acting like big boys, Blake, Peter and I played from the tips (Ha!). The par 5 2nd hole plays downhill and was reachable for Peter. Blake and I layed up and it was a wise move. The green is L-shaped, and the pin location was difficult with anything more than a wedge in your hand. The bunkers are visually intimidating but are relatively easy to get up and down.

Course: Fox Run
Type: Public
Website: foxrungolf.org
Location: Ludlow, VT
Phone: (802) 228-1396
Par 70. Yardage Played 6540 (Black)
Rating: 71.4/131

The par 3 8th is a spectacular downhill 187-yard par 3. The drop is more than 50 feet meaning it plays more like 140 yards. The views of the ski resort, the mountains and the trees in the distance is stunning. The short par 4 10th (308 yards the day we played) offers the opportunity to be a hero but the bunkers and water make the risk very real. The 400-yard 12th was fantastic with a tunnel to hit through off the tee. It also has a stream crossing the fairway diagonally forcing a decision on club selection and requiring supreme execution to be able to hit the green and not go into the water.

Me, Blake and Peter on the 17th Tee

The two par threes on the back nine, 14 and 17, are long carries over the water (both are over 200 yards). Very picturesque holes that need a better photographer than me to do them justice. Overall, a fabulous course with great views. The three par 5's and five par 3's challenge all golfers and the very short but tight par 4 10th will test your strategic thinking. Fox Run has several elevation changes requiring thoughtful club selection. The greens are outstanding with great pace and lots of undulations. Look up "hidden gem" in the dictionary and you would find Fox Run. If you are trying to play golf in all 50 states and need Vermont, I recommend that you enjoy Fox Run

Views from Fox Run

227

Scenes from Fox Run

Virginia

Virginia is for lovers, as the saying goes, but for golfers if you aren't at a private club or a resort like the Omni Homestead, it's a crap shoot. Flying into Dulles airport was always interesting. I traveled to the Reston area for business in the early 1990s and played a couple of the local daily fee courses. Reston National was considered a gem at the time, but it was mediocre at best, and reading recent reviews on GolfNow, it has gone further downhill since.

Course: Reston National
Type: Public
Website:
https://www.restonnationalgc.com
Location: Reston, VA
Phone: (703) 620-9333
Par 71. Yardage Played 6479 (Black)
Rating: 71.1/128

Reston National opened in 1970. Designed by Ed Ault, the course features 18 thoughtfully crafted holes that cater to golfers of all skill levels. With strategic bunkering, water features, and undulating terrain, the course presents a variety of shots that test your skills and decision-making. Reston National is a parkland layout and certified Audubon Cooperative Sanctuary. The Audubon Cooperative Sanctuary Program for Golf is an education and certification program that helps golf courses protect the environment and preserve the natural heritage of the game. By helping people enhance the valuable natural areas and wildlife habitats that golf courses provide, improve efficiency, and minimize potentially harmful impacts of golf course operations, the program serves an important environmental role worldwide.

Reston National is heavily wooded. It has with fairly large greens and wide fairways. The course plays over 6,800 yards from the back tees to a par of 71. I played it from one set up (black tees) and was paired with a couple from Richmond who were visiting family. We played as a threesome, very slowly. I enjoyed the course, but it was nothing very memorable. It was in good shape, it is easy to get to from Dulles airport, and the staff was friendly. The fairways are nice and the rough can be penal, but it won't crush you. There is a nice mix of strategy and length required, but if you manage the course and are moderately accurate it's a fair test. There are no blind shots or gimmicks. The par 3s were all the same playing 160-170 yards, would like to see at least one short one (less than 130) and one long one (200+) to test all parts of the game. The bunkering was very predictable and not difficult.

Scenes from Reston National

As you step onto the tee box of the 3rd hole at Reston National Golf Club, you're greeted by a rolling fairway and strategically placed bunkers. This 400-yard par 4, aptly named "Tranquil

Meadows," presents a serene experience. The fairway gently slopes downhill, tempting you to try to bomb a drive that will leave you with a short approach to the green. However, the fairway narrows as it approaches the green, demanding precision off the tee. Strategic bunker placements on both sides of the fairway and near the green introduce a calculated risk-reward dynamic. The approach shot requires careful consideration, as the green is guarded by a small pond to the left and a series of bunkers to the right. The undulating green adds an extra layer of complexity, making the putt a true test of your green-reading skills. Hole 3 at Reston National is a visual and tactical challenge.

Hole 16 – "Water's Edge" stands as a picturesque 190-yard par 3 that embodies both the scenic beauty and challenge that define Reston National Golf Club. The hole plays downhill but demands precision. The water hazard poses a challenge as you must carry the ball over the pond to reach the green. Bunkers positioned to the right of the green further intensify the pressure of a well-placed shot. The undulating green adds an element of intrigue to the putting challenge that awaits. As you stand on the tee, taking in the view of the water and the surrounding nature, you'll find yourself captivated by the beauty and the shot-making demands of this par 3.

Playing from a bunker at Reston National

Washington

The state motto of Washington is "Alki" a Native American Chinook word that means "bye and bye," "I will see you again," "future hope," or "eventually." The motto Alki comes from a group of early settlers from New York who named their new settlement "New York" in honor of the east coast's great city. This new settlement did not experience such booming growth, however, and was renamed "New York Alki" or "Alki Point, New York" in hopes that the territory would eventually prosper. Alki Point later developed into what is now Seattle. The state motto of Washington is the only motto of all 50 states to remain unofficial. Alki is how I feel about golfing in Washington. We did a buddies' trip to Gold Mountain, Chambers Bay, and The Home Course a few years ago and hopefully I will see them again.

The Olympic course at Gold Mountain is one of the premier public courses in Washington and an outstanding municipal facility. The John Harbottle design opened in 1996 and features towering evergreens, a handful of water hazards, and significant elevation changes. It stands as one of the best value courses you will ever come across. The finishing holes, 16-18 provide a fun and excellent test with a long par 3 over water (188 yards), a gargantuan par 4 through the trees (470 yards) and a short par 4 (325 yards) to make birdie to finish.

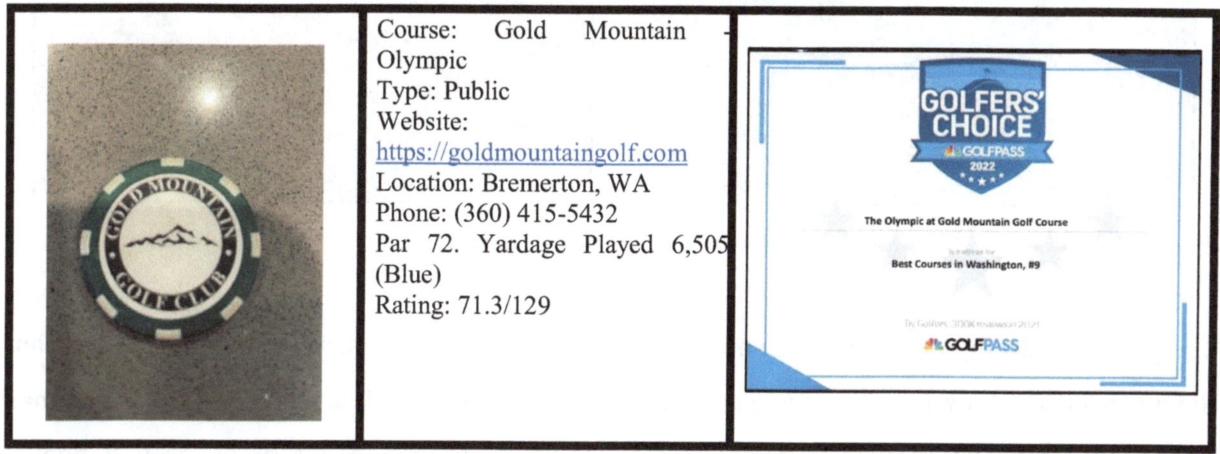

Course: Gold Mountain - Olympic
Type: Public
Website: https://goldmountaingolf.com
Location: Bremerton, WA
Phone: (360) 415-5432
Par 72. Yardage Played 6,505 (Blue)
Rating: 71.3/129

The Olympic Course at Gold Mountain

The Home Course is cooperatively owned and operated by the Pacific Northwest Golf Association (PNGA) and Washington Golf (WA Golf). It hosts PNGA Championships and is very golfer friendly. It has stunning views and is a fun course to play. Unfortunately for us, we were there just a couple of days after aeration and the greens were not in great shape. The layout, however, was very fun.

Views from The Home Course

The gem of Washington state, in my opinion, is Chambers Bay. Robert Trent Jones II and team did a masterful job routing the course and making it enjoyable for all levels of golfers. This links style course offers an infinite number of ways to play it … through the air, on the ground, hooks, cuts, putter from 30 yards or a flop shot if it is in your bag. It is fun! We played Chambers Bay a couple years after Jordan Spieth won the US Open after Dustin Johnson three-putted from 8 feet

233

on the 72nd hole. The US Open trophy was still there, so we had to have our picture taken with it in the pro shop.

Me, Norm and Bart with the US Open Trophy at Chambers Bay

Chambers Bay is a rock quarry covered in sand, the course sits down in a giant bowl bordered by the railroad and Puget Sound on the west. It is a true links course that has no interior water hazards, only one single tree (that is out of play but very picturesque), and virtually no place to lose a ball. The huge, undulated greens compliment the expansive fairways that sprawl around the large sand dunes and bunkering systems. Firm and fast conditions are the call of the day with the sandy soil that features a combination of bent and fescue grasses. This grass combination never gets very plush which allows for players to advance the ball on the ground and utilize the contours of the terrain. This type of grass also requires the course to be walking only as it cannot sustain the extra strain put on it by consistent golf cart traffic. As such, caddies are available, and I highly recommend using them.

Course: Chambers Bay
Type: Public
Website:
https://www.chambersbaygolf.com
Location: Bremerton, WA
Phone: (877) 295-4657
Par 72. Yardage Played 6,586 (Sand)
Rating: 71.9/130

The 7th hole is one of my favorites, "Humpback", is a long uphill par 4 turns hard from left to right. Hitting your tee shot over the bunker on the right invites a shorter approach to the green, but also brings trouble into play. Going left off the tee leaves a blind approach over the humps fronting the green. The uphill approach plays much longer than the actual yardage.

Walking down #7 Fairway

The 15th hole has the only tree on the property which stands behind a large green and next to the 16th tee. The most photographed hole on the course features a large bunker complex in the foreground and the glistening Puget Sound in the background. While we played it from 140, there are additional tees that can stretch this hole all the way back to 250 yards! A tongue in front and spilling to the right feed balls away from the hole and possibly into a sprawling bunker surrounding three-quarters of the green. Back left of the green is a small pot bunker that is devilish and should be avoided at all costs.

Views of the 15th Hole at Chambers Bay, Kevin and Craig putting

Chamber's Basement, Don't go here

My caddy at Chambers Bay asked me not to hit my driver down the middle of the fairway on 18, "Tahoma". Having a serious lack of talent, I ripped it down the middle and heard a huge groan from my caddy. I was in "Chambers Basement." It is the 10-foot-deep pot bunker in the middle of the 18th fairway at Chambers Bay, 120 yards from the center of the green. Splashed the ball out, hit a wedge on and two putted for bogey on one of the easier holes on the course, if you avoid the basement and don't three putt like Dustin Johnson. Oh well.

Views at Chambers Bay

West Virginia

West Virginia is known for coal mines (most in the United States, 151) and trees (the Monongahela National Forest covers nearly a million acres of land and spans across 10 counties). The Mountain State also houses the Green Bank Telescope. The Green Bank Telescope picks up radio transmissions from outer space, and even the tiniest interference can make it impossible to decipher what those radio waves from space mean. No cell phones and no Wi-Fi make this part of West Virginia truly unique in today's modern world.

West Virginia is home to some wonderful properties. The Greenbrier is consistently rated one of the best resorts in America and, as the home of Sam Snead, some fantastic golf. Unfortunately, I was not able to play there on my quest. Instead, I drove a couple of hours west from Baltimore and played at Oglebay Resort near Wheeling WV.

Course: Oglebay Resort - Jones
Type: Resort
Website: https://oglebay.com
Location: Wheeling, WA
Phone: (304) 243-4050
Par 71. Yardage Played 6,605 (Blue)
Rating: 72.1/132

Oglebay has two courses, one Arnold Palmer Signature design and one Robert Trent Jones, Sr. course. I played the Jones course because of a tournament being held on the Palmer course. The Jones course was built in 1970 and has a lot of slopes off the mountain with deep rough about 15 yards off a fairway, usually resulting in a lost ball. For reference, I have a picture of my driver next to the rough on the second hole! The rough climbs more than 1/4 the way up the shaft. It requires a lot of local knowledge to play well and even more to score with some unforgiving greens. The course hosted the West Virginia LPGA Classic for 11 years in the 1970s and 1980s, and the ladies and their caddies certainly had a workout. The West Virginia state open was played here once ... in 2009… not sure if they will be back, competition rounds could take forever on this course.

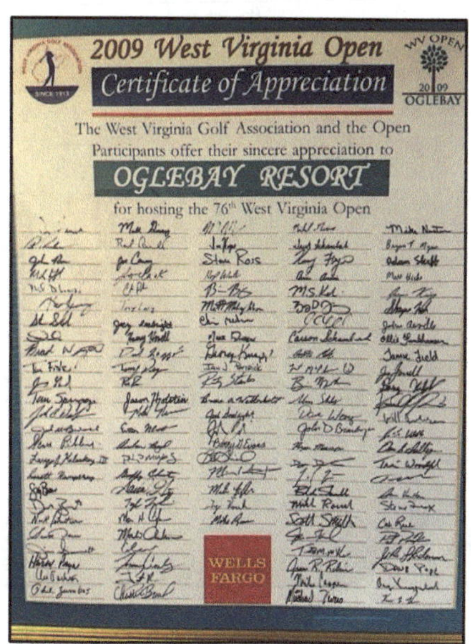

The rough is deep for the players in the West Virginia Open

I was paired with two great guys, brothers-in-laws, Paul and Brad. Paul was a big guy that hit it a ton off the tee. Brad was about the same as me distance-wise. He was retired from NiSource and a recreational golfer. It was mid-October, we imagined the weather would be cool, but nice. We were wrong! It was 37 degrees when we teed off, well below my personal minimum playing temperature of 44 degrees Fahrenheit… maybe it would warm up. Wrong again! It began to drizzle on the 5th hole, a sharp dogleg right par 5, then the snow came. It snowed beginning with the second shot on the 5th and through the sixth hole. It stopped on the 7th, a 230-yard uphill par 3 and warmed up to about 40 degrees for the rest of the round. Luckily the wind was slight, 5-10 mph out of the north. BRRRH ... for a boy who has been in Texas for 30 years. The key mantra for this round… "Swing Easy and Except the Extra the Distance."

The course was well maintained and a serious challenge for golfers of all skill levels. There were 5 sets of tees making it playable for everyone. The cups were all pink, which was fun, and navigating the tree lines along with key water hazards forced serious thought on a number of shots.

Views from the Jones Course at Oglebay Resort

October at the Jones Course

Views of the Sloping Fairways and Greens

Almost a year after playing I received a text message from Brad and Paul, they were back at Oglebay with much nicer weather and enjoying their round. This text message reminded me once again that 90% of golf is who you play with.

Wisconsin

Wisconsin is the dairy capital of the United States, producing more milk than any other state. It is also home to 15,210 miles of signed and groomed snowmobile trails as well as the largest cross country skiing event in North America, The American Birkebeiner, a 52K cross-country ski race between Cable and Hayward. Winter sports are big in Wisconsin.

Wisconsin is also home to an incredible number of excellent golf courses including six ranked in the Golf Digest 200: Whistling Straits, Erin Hills, Sand Valley, Blackwolf Run, Mammoth Dunes, and Milwaukee Country Club. My good friend Kevin and I played in the 2020 Sand Valley Cup together. We drove from Austin, Texas to Sand Valley because our original plan of flying to Chicago and driving from there was thwarted by COVID and the quarantine in place at O'Hare.

Our Head Pro with My Friend Kevin and Me and our Member/Member Championship Plaques

The Sand Valley Cup was four days of wonderful golf starting with an afternoon round at The Sandbox, exceptional executive short course designed by Coore and Crenshaw. I surprisingly won a closest to the pin during this event and was awarded a ball marker engraved with my initials.

Course: Sand Valley
Type: Resort
Website: https://sandvalley.com
Location: Nekoosa, WI
Phone: (888) 651-5539
  Par 72. Sand Valley 6,514 yards
  played (orange). 71.4/130
  Par 73. Mammoth Dunes 6,516
  yards played. (orange) 70.5/124
  Sandbox 1,652

Sand Valley is an excellent course to challenge all parts of your game. Mammoth Dunes was designed by David McLay Kidd. It has a cool logo. The course itself is wide open and fun to play. It is interesting in that it is a par 73 course with five par 5 holes but only four par 3 holes on the card. My caddie, Austin Benz, told me he had shot 58 there. The best I could do was 76. Austin is a pretty good player. We stayed on property in one of the cabana rooms near the par three course, and met a lot of wonderful people during the event. We introduced a group of guys from Iowa to the "Deuce Club" and enjoyed taking their money by making a few 2's during the event.

Tee Shots at Mammoth Dunes and Sand Valley

The "Deuce Club" is a game started by the boys in Maine and introduced to us in Texas during a winter trip to Florida. You must "join" the Deuce Club by making a two in the presence of at least one deuce club member. If the member invites you to join after your deuce, you must pay all Deuce Club members in your group (usually a foursome) $2 to join. From that point on, any time you make a 2 (whether it is on a par 3, 4, or 5) you get $2 from each Deuce Club member playing in your group that day. We have roughly 40 members in the Deuce Club at our courses in Texas, but we know of about 20 in Maine and after this event at Sand Valley there are at least 8 more in Iowa.

Since we were driving and it was COVID, we decided to head over to Erin Hills to spend a night and play at a major championship venue the next day. Wow! What a great decision. Erin Hills was in pristine condition; the bar was awesome and the accommodations on property were quaint. We had a wonderful evening sipping scotch by the fire and putting on the enormous putting green until it was dark.

Views at Sand Valley

Erin Hills was deigned by Michael Hurdzan, Dana Fry, and Ron Whitten. It can stretch to 8,300 yards.. It is a enormous property that is a long walk. Caddies are key. Unfortunately for our group, the weather came in on 16 and all caddies were called off the course, so we carried our bags on the last three holes and just beat the rain. We were told that Dustin Johnson holds the course record "from the 8,300-yard tips" at 80. There is no way to verify this, because the course is never played at that length, but it sounds high to me. There is really not a lot of trouble on the course, it is just really really long. I think Dustin Johnson, Brooks Koepka and Rory McIlory could all easily break 80 from the tips.

Course: Erin Hills
Type: Public
Website: https://erinhills.com
Location: Erin, WI
Phone: (866) 772-4769
Par 72. Yardage Played 6,491 (Green/White Combination)
Rating: 72.0/132

Lodging at Erin Hills

I hope to make it to Koehler soon to finish off the Wisconsin "Best of" and add at least a few more Major Championship venues to my list.

Fun before Teeing off

Views during the round at Erin Hills

"Links Style" golf in Wisconsin

Wyoming

Wyoming is known for Oil, Ranches and Yellowstone National Park. It was the first U.S. State to give women the right to vote and goes by the moniker of "The Equality State." Cheyenne hosts the Frontier Days Rodeo which is considered "The Granddaddy of them all." Devils Tower and Old Faithful are famous landmarks most people are familiar with in Wyoming. Sheridan, Wyoming is a wonderful town about 120 miles south of Billings, Montana near Yellowstone National Park.

The Powder horn Golf Club is a private club with 27 holes designed by Dick Bailey. Woods and wetlands surround the Old Red Barn to create target golf with Old West flair on the Stag Nine. The Eagle Nine rounds out the course, offering surprising length and creative shots within a mix of meadow and creek-side terrain. With a nod to the game's mecca, The Old Course at St. Andrews, the Mountain Nine features a small replica of the famous Swilcan Bridge, as well as large greens, 30 sizeable sand bunkers and the open rolling terrain of a Scottish links course.

We were on a buddies' trip that started with a trip to the College World Series in Omaha, Nebraska. We drove to play Sand Hills in Mullen, NE, then up to South Dakota to Mount Rushmore, Sturgis and The Golf Club at Red Rock. From there it was on to Bully Pulpit in North Dakota and over to Yellowstone Country Club in Billings. This is where things got interesting. Our friend, who hosted us at Yellowstone Country Club, encouraged us to play The Powder Horn in Sheridan. We had planned to go to Yellowstone National Park, but the entrance was closed because of flooding. As we drank bourbon and scotch in the bar in Billings, we discussed making the drive to Sheridan. So, I hopped online to get us a tee time. A quick search for Powder Horn Golf Club provided a link to make tee times (turns out the "THE" in "The Powder Horn" is important), so I got one at 1:30 the next afternoon and proudly told the guys, it looks like it is a done deal $35/man. We all went to bed very pleased.

The next morning, we woke up to drive the 90 minutes to The Powder Horn (the speed limit is 80). As we pulled into the subdivision there were enormous 10,000 square foot houses and amazing views. You could see the course between the gaps and Peter remarked, "George, this doesn't look like a $35 golf course." I replied. "I know, it looks incredible!"

After we parked, we went into the club house where Blake informed the assistant pro behind the counter "We're the Stark group and we have a 1:30 tee time." The young assistant looked at Blake perplexed and commented, "Sir, we are private club, no outside play without an accompanied member." Blake looked at me and said, "George, didn't you make a tee time?" I said, "Yes." And handed the assistant my phone with this confirmation number and booking. He studied it for a moment and gave me a blank stare. I said "Wrong day or wrong time?" He replied, "Wrong Time Zone. This course is in Chicago."… Oops!

Course: The Powder horn –
Stag/Eagle
Type: Private
Website:
https://www.thepowderhorn.com
Location: Sheridan, WY
Phone: (307) 673-4800
Par 72. Yardage Played 6,725 (Middle)
Rating: 71.8/130

About this time, the head pro came out from his office laughing having heard the exchange. He asked, "Are you guys' members of a private club?", we all replied to the affirmative. He asked about our head pro, and we told him, and he said, "Oh, I know Aaron." Tell you what, we will let you on for the guest rate. We asked, "How much is the guest fee?" He responded with "$125." The course was a bargain. We all had a good laugh and headed to the range.

We chose the middle tees and the course provided plenty of challenge. The Dick Bailey designed course takes advantage of the plentiful water, angles, narrow landing areas, and well placed bunkers to protect itself and force you to use a full regiment of clubs; the elevation and thin air make it play a little shorter than the posted yardage. There are a few "driver/wedge" holes to be had here, but the mix of yardages with elevation changes is outstanding. I also liked the variety in both the par 5's (ranging from a reachable 485 to a big boy 603 yard challenge) and the par 3's (from a wedge to a four iron). Again, The Powder Horn means to test your full game.

The greens appeared straight forward and seemed easy to play; however, after a quick three putt and watching a putt break 3 feet when I played 4 inches, suggested the greens were a little tougher than I gave them credit for on the putting green. In either case they were well maintained and rolled true, arguably a bigger factor in scoring well than how much break might they contain.

Our 10th hole was the #1 on the Stag 9, the sound of the river near the tee and the beauty of the hole. It is a shorter par 4 (just 310 from the blues) with trees and water down the left side preventing a direct route to the green without a towering missle. Since we did not have the ability to fire missles, we laid up and each hit little wedges onto the green. My lone birdie of the day. Some holes are meant to be managed rather than attacked head on, and doing so can lead to a good score; this is such a hole.

Number 4 on the Eagle course, needed to be met head on. It was a long par 4 playing 425 with water bisecting the fairway in two places. It required a long, well-placed tee shot and a mid-iron into a smallish green. Very pretty hole and fun to play. My favorite par 5 was our 12th hole, the 3rd on the Stag Nine. It plays 530 with a wide landing zone off the tee with a bunker on the right with deep native grasses on the left. The second shot must carry a series of ponds that split the fairway into two parts. A short approach to a fabulous green complex leaves a real birdie opportunity.

If you can get on The Powder Horn, I highly recommend that you do it.

Views from The Powder Horn

Views from the Powder Horn

Final Thoughts

Playing golf in all 50 United States is a rewarding journey for any avid golfer. Here are some final thoughts and reflections on my odyssey:

1. **Diverse Golfing Experiences**: The United States offers an incredible range of golf courses, from scenic coastal links to challenging mountain layouts and rolling desert fairways. Playing in all 50 states exposes you to a variety of golfing experiences and landscapes. I will make it back to a few of the states where I only got in one round, especially Tennessee, Rhode Island and West Virginia. They deserve more attention. I will make it to Kohler and to Big Cedar Lodge, two resorts that get high praise and look like great fun.

2. **Time and Commitment:** Playing golf in all 50 states is a significant commitment in terms of time and resources. Planning and logistics, as well as managing your time to accommodate such an adventure, can be challenging. It has taken me 50 years of golfing to complete playing golf in all 50 states, but the majority were done in the last three years.

4. **Connecting with Nature and Culture:** Golfing in different states allows you to appreciate the natural beauty of the United States. You may encounter wildlife, stunning landscapes, and various weather conditions that add to the golfing experience. My friends and I have made some long trips to complete this journey. Some by car and some via air, then by car. My friends taught me the value of stopping to enjoy other landmarks along way (Mt. Rushmore, Basketball and Football Hall of Fames, Boston Red Sox, Budweiser Brewery, Alaska Conservation Society and Graceland) were all great experiences. These side trips break up the golf and provide fun conversation when we are on the road home.

5. **Skill Improvement:** Challenging courses and varying conditions can help improve your golf skills. Remember, Swing Easy and Accept the Extra Distance. You'll have the chance to adapt to different grasses, terrains and elements, which can make you a more versatile and skilled player. It emphasized to me how good the players on the Professional Tours are going from location to location and still shooting low scores. Incredible.

6. **Lifelong Memories:** Each round of golf in a new state offers the opportunity to create unique memories and stories that you'll cherish for years to come. The stories in this book highlight many of my favorites.

7. **Challenges and Obstacles:** You may face logistical challenges, such as travel, cost, and course availability. Weather conditions can also be unpredictable, especially in some states (See West Virginia and Oklahoma), making golfing a test of adaptability.

8. **Golfing Community:** Engaging with the golfing community across the country can be enriching. You'll meet fellow golfers with shared interests and perhaps even make lifelong friends along the way. I enjoyed my friends and family and new acquaintances that I met playing golf on this odyssey. Meeting colorful characters across the United States adds fun to every golf journey and getting paired with random golfers can add some great stories to anyone's portfolio.

9. **Golf Ratings are Flawed**: I have also learned not to trust the ratings that are published or to skip over small town municipal courses. I have played some highly rated courses by the experts and some courses that will never be rated. A few of the highly rated courses did not meet expectations and I learned that expensive is not always better.

In conclusion, playing golf in all 50 states is NOT a monumental undertaking, I just decided to go. With that decision came incredible experiences, personal growth, and lifelong memories. It required some planning, dedication, and a passion for the game. It's a journey that connects you with the diversity and beauty of the United States, both on and off the golf course.

90% of Golf is Who You Play With

TEE TO GREEN
A GOLFER'S ODYSSEY THROUGH AMERICA'S 50 STATES

Traveling across the United States to play golf is a dream come true for avid golfers and adventure seekers alike. The country boasts an array of stunning golf courses, from Bandon Dunes on the rugged Oregon coast to the beautifully restored Bellaire Country Club on the Florida Gulf. Each course offers a unique blend of natural beauty and challenging play.

In this captivating journey, golf enthusiast and author George Stark takes you on an odyssey through all 50 states, showcasing the incredible diversity and uniqueness of golf courses from coast to coast. From iconic, world-renowned courses (Sand Hills, Pinehurst) to hidden gems off the beaten path (Fox Run, Bully Pulpit), George recounts anecdotes from the journey and describes favorite holes from the courses he visited. Hopefully this will inspire you to make the journey and create memories with friends and new acquaintances.

"90% of Golf is who you play with."

ABOUT THE AUTHOR

George Stark spent more than thirty years as a research scientist for NASA and IBM. He is a low handicap golfer that enjoys traveling to play courses across the world. He was certified as a course rater by the Texas Golf Association and has played more than 500 courses in the United States and in 11 countries.